Your Livin

D0286168

Your Living Compass

Living Well in Thought, Word, and Deed

SCOTT STONER

Morehouse Publishing
NEW YORK · HARRISBURG · DENVER

Unless otherwise noted, the Scripture quotations contained herein are from the New Revised Standard Version Bible, copyright © 1989 by the Division of Christian Education of the National Council of Churches of Christ in the U.S.A. Used by permission. All rights reserved.

Quotations from the Episcopal Book of Common Prayer (BCP) are from the 1979 edition, published by Church Hymnal Corporation, New York, NY.

Morehouse Publishing
4785 Linglestown Road, Suite 101, Harrisburg, PA 17112

Morehouse Publishing
19 East 34th Street, New York, NY 10016

Morehouse Publishing is an imprint of Church Publishing Incorporated.
www.churchpublishing.org

The Living Compass Self-Assessment Tool is available online at
www.churchpublishing.org/yourlivingcompass.

Cover design by Laurie Klein Westhafer
Typeset by Vicki K. Black

Library of Congress Cataloging-in-Publication Data
Stoner, Scott.
Your living compass : living well in thought, word, and deed / Scott Stoner.
    pages   cm
ISBN 978-0-8192-2940-3 (pbk.) -- ISBN 978-0-8192-2941-0 (ebook)
1. Christian life. 2. Spiritual life. 3. Spiritual retreats. I. Title.
BV4501.3.S7626 2014
248.4--dc23

                              2014004735

CONTENTS

Jeffrey D. Lee

FOREWORD

In our work together with Scott and Holly Stoner and the Living Compass ministries in the Episcopal Diocese of Chicago we often use this phrase: "What you focus on grows." Whether in our task of cultivating congregational vitality, or encouraging the formation of wellness groups among individuals across congregational lines, or working with ministry partners beyond the official boundaries of the Episcopal Church, our conviction is that where we focus our attention determines to a large extent just how significant any particular aspect of our life will become. Nowhere is this more evident than in the creation of healthy, growing, spiritually deepening communities of Christians. Congregations are made up, after all, of individual members; if we focus on the health and wellness of those individuals in community, the community as a whole tends to flourish. If we allow our focus to become transfixed by systemic dysfunction and scarcity, those things seem to grow too.

I have known Scott Stoner and counted him as a colleague for over twenty years, first in his role as a therapist with a particular care for the wellness and recovery issues of clergy and then as a priest and colleague in ministry. Scott and I followed each other in serving as Rector of St. Christopher's Church in the Diocese of Milwaukee, a congregation that grew through a significant period of conflict into an extraordinarily vibrant and growing community. And now we are colleagues again in the Diocese of Chicago where I serve as bishop and Scott serves as the director of an exciting new initiative called the Nicholas Center, a place of ministry devoted to developing transformational leadership in the church for the sake of the world. The Nicholas Center hosts a number of programs for groups of leaders and is the headquarters for Living Compass, a faith and wellness initiative founded by Scott and his wife Holly. Living Compass provides training programs for clergy and lay leaders who come from across the country to the Nicholas Center to be trained as certified Living Compass Congregational Wellness Advocates. This ministry grows out of their work as Christian leaders, teachers, and skilled therapists, and is based on their commitment to the principle that what you focus on in life does indeed grow. They are eyewitnesses to the truth of it.

Jesus told his first friends that he had come to give people abundant life (John 10:10). Too often it seems we reduce that promise into an expectation of simply getting by. This spiritual issue is mirrored in much of our approach to healthcare in the United States. Scott has remarked to me more than once that he believes what we have in this country is not so much a healthcare system as a disease management system. On a graphic scale first developed in the medical field and used in the Living Compass program, wellness can be portrayed as a continuum between extreme illness and death on the one hand and resilient health and vitality on the other.

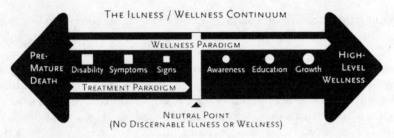

A great deal of medical care does seem to be focused on the center of the graph. We often aim at homeostasis as though that were the goal. Now, surely the center is preferable to the disease side of things, but why isn't our focus on moving more deeply into the realm of vibrancy and abundant health? Obviously, medicating symptoms is often important, but there is so much more to us than any particular manifestation of disease. Why settle for a narrow focus? The work of Living Compass is based on the conviction that this question is just as important for our hearts and souls as it is for our physical bodies. It embraces the human person holistically: heart, soul, strength, and mind. This holistic focus on abundant living is equally important for the communities where we live and practice our faith and from which we reach out to the needs and hungers and hurts of the world. The Living Compass and similar initiatives are a gift to the church, aimed squarely at what the letter to the Ephesians describes as the body, "building itself up in love" (Ephesians 4:16).

In leading wellness groups or Living Compass retreats Scott will sometimes begin by describing what the Living Compass is not. It is not a self-help program, not "ten steps to a better you!" Instead, it offers a way simply to pay attention to your life, to note what is most alive and growing, and what needs to be nurtured and tended for the sake of the abundant life Jesus promises. This book is a guide, a resource or tool for that work. Here is a retreat to help you pay attention, to focus on wellness. It will be a useful gift for any individual or group longing for a more abundant, balanced, vibrant life.

WELCOME TO THIS RETREAT

Wellness is a popular topic these days. Wellness programs are now common in the workplace, in high schools, at colleges and universities, in community centers, and in many retirement communities. Much has been written about the topic of wellness, including countless books and the very popular wellness blog "Well" in the *New York Times*. A great deal of individual and societal benefit has come about as a result of this current emphasis on wellness programs and wellness education.

So why is there a need for one more book about wellness? Because this book approaches wellness from a unique perspective, focusing on the integration of wellness and Christian spirituality. It is about the integration of ancient spiritual principles and modern understandings of wellness. It is a book that will help the reader discover the ancient Christian roots of many modern approaches to wellness.

Most approaches to wellness, both ancient and modern, begin with inviting individuals to pull back from their everyday routine and reflect in a more intentional manner about the choices they are making. In both ancient and modern times, one way to create this time and space is to go on some type of a retreat. The word "retreat," when used as a verb, means to pull back, and that is exactly what this book will invite you to do—to create some time and space to pull back from your everyday routine and reflect more deeply on the choices you are making in several areas of wellness.

Some readers may have a very positive association to the word retreat, while others may be turned off by the idea, thinking of a retreat as something that is religious or "churchy." I hope that you will instead find the self-guided retreat format of this book to be a welcome opportunity to pull back and to do a bit of reflecting on what matters most in your life. I hope you will come to think of creating some retreat time in your life as a simple gift that you can give yourself any time you need to catch your breath and pull back from the busy demands of your life.

Going on a Retreat

If you ask people if they would like to have some time to slow down the pace of their lives, reflect on what truly matters to them, and then refocus their life based on that self-reflection, I would guess that most would answer affirmatively. There are many ways to create time for self-reflection and refocusing. There is one specific way that has been around for thousands of years and that is to go on a retreat.

Going on a retreat is a unique kind of experience. While it may involve a change in location, it is very different from a vacation. Unlike a vacation, the primary purpose of a retreat is to create time for introspection, self-reflection, and refocusing. Retreat time can also involve a planning component, as for example when a leadership group of any kind goes on a retreat to focus on strategic planning. Finally, many retreats have a strong spiritual focus, creating time and space for participants to connect more deeply with God.

Retreats are a perfect response to the pace of modern living; they are also, in fact, an ancient practice. Moses retreated to Mount Sinai. Jesus retreated to the desert and created time away to pray on a regular basis. Buddhists, Hindus, Muslims, and Native Americans regularly take retreats. Retreats allow time to delve beneath the surface of one's life. Retreats invite us into a deeper encounter with both the light and the shadow within ourselves.

While it is easy to recognize the many benefits of going on a retreat, it is also easy to recognize the common barriers to engaging in such an experience. The primary barrier for many people is not having the time to go away for an extended period of self-reflection and renewal. Not knowing where to go, or not having easy access to a retreat program are other challenges a person might face. A prohibitive factor for others can be the cost of a retreat.

These barriers are real and prevent many people from experiencing the positive and profound effects that can come from going on a retreat. For that reason, I am delighted to be able to offer you this self-guided retreat that intentionally overcomes all of these barriers. This retreat can be experienced in just fifteen minutes a day either on your own in the privacy of your own home or with others. If you prefer to experience this retreat with others you may want to organize a group to meet at each others' homes, at a coffee shop, or as small group or education program in connection with your church or faith community.

This book offers you a chance to experience each of the following aspects of a traditional retreat in a self-guided retreat format, at your own pace either by yourself or with others. You will be invited to reflect on eight areas of wellness in your life. The retreat will offer you a process that will take you to a different place within your own heart and soul. It provides a collection of reflections that will invite you to do some deeper introspection and self-reflection regarding your wellness. There will also be opportunity for you to do some strategic planning regarding your life balance and the choices you are making in eight different areas of wellness. Finally, this book will help you nurture your faith and strengthen your connection with God's presence in your life.

Who Can Benefit from this Self-Guided Retreat?

Many people can benefit from this retreat. Here is a description of the kinds of people who might find this retreat helpful. Perhaps you will find yourself in one or several of these descriptions.

- ◆ You may be a person who feels your life is out of balance, or who feels a growing uneasiness in your life, your relationships, or in your work. Stress, anxiety, or worry may be taking hold of you and you want to do something about that. You may be hoping that this retreat will help restore balance in your life and reduce some of the uneasiness you are experiencing.

- ◆ You may be a person who describes yourself as "spiritual, but not religious." Your spirituality is important to you, but you are not sure where you fit when it comes to organized religion. Perhaps you have been hurt by or had a bad experience with organized religion and are wondering if it can ever play a meaningful role in your life. If this is the case, I hope this book will provide some healing for you and possibly provide a bridge to a new, more positive experience of Christian community. While this retreat is grounded in and grows out of a Christian context, you do not have to be Christian to find meaning and value in it.

- ◆ You may be a person who is very active in your church or faith community. Your faith is an important compass in your life, and you might be seeking a deeper understanding of the connection between faith and wellness. You may be hoping that this retreat will help you deepen the ways in which your faith can serve as a compass in all aspects of your life.

- ◆ You may be a person who has tried a number of personal growth and wellness programs. Perhaps you are looking for something more than what these other programs offered,

desiring an approach to wellness that is more holistic. You may
be hoping that the approach to wellness in this retreat will lead
to more satisfying and sustaining changes in your life.

◆ You may be a faith leader, lay or ordained, looking for a
resource to strengthen the wellness of people within your
congregation. This retreat can be used by any congregation as
either a small group program or an adult education program.
You may also be looking for a wellness resource that you can
use as a way to reach out to people in your community who
are not members of your congregation.

Wherever you find yourself in the options above, you are welcome here.
And wherever you find yourself in regard to your personal wellness and
your spiritual journey, you are welcome here. I am glad you have found
this self-guided retreat and I hope it will be a valuable resource for enhancing your wellness and for creating a more abundant life.

Your Retreat Facilitator

For more than thirty years, I have had the honor of walking with people
on their journeys toward healing and wellness. I have walked with people
in my professional life as an Episcopal priest, psychotherapist, retreat
leader, and spiritual director, and in my personal life as a husband, father,
and friend. Within all of these relationships, I have walked as a fellow traveler on the life-long journey toward wellness.

A few years ago I made a renewed commitment to turn my attention
and work to the connection between the Christian faith and wellness. The
fruit of this work has been the creation of the Living Compass Faith and
Wellness Initiative. This book is a part of that initiative. The Living Compass Faith and Wellness Initiative provides a variety of educational and
coaching resources to assist individuals, families, and congregations to be
well in heart, soul, strength, and mind. Recently, Living Compass has created training opportunities for those who wish to become certified Congregational Wellness Advocates.

Foundational for all the work I have done as a priest and psychotherapist is a quotation from an early church leader by the name of Irenaeus,
who wrote in the second century, "The glory of God is a human being fully
alive."* To be fully alive is to be fully who God intends us to be with
all of the joy, sorrow, and vulnerability that define who we are as human
beings.

I have been leading retreats my entire professional life designed to help
people feel fully alive. I have led retreats for people of all ages and from

* *Adversus Haereses* (Against Heresies), 4.34.5–7.

every walk of life. Many of the retreats have focused on emotional and spiritual wellness, others on couple and family wellness. I have also led retreats that have provided support for people recovering from addictions, as well as people recovering from loss of a relationship or the loss of a loved one through death. There is no other way to say it: I love leading retreats that support people as they strive to heal, grow, and become fully alive!

I am honored and delighted to now share this book, this compass. Whether you do this retreat on your own or with others, I hope and pray that you will experience wanted growth and a better understanding of where you want to go on this journey we call life, and that you will feel more fully alive. And in the end, that is all that matters. This book is simply a compass to help guide you on your journey.

I have been on many journeys in the wilds of Canada where the compass I used was essential in helping me to find my way. When I returned from those journeys, though, the stories I told were not about how great the compass was. The stories instead were about the transformative experiences I had on my journey. I hope your journey through this retreat will be the same for you. This book, which serves as your compass, along with other tools you find here, will be helpful, but they are just tools. In the end what will matter most is your willingness to go on this journey and to be transformed.

Living Well: A Combination of Thought, Word, and Deed

The concept of living well in thought, word, and deed is central to this book. Our thoughts, words, and deeds are all interrelated, each part affecting the others. Our thoughts influence our words and deeds. Our words, both what we say and do not say, influence our thoughts and deeds. And our deeds, our actions, shape our thoughts and words. Everything is interconnected.

Each reflection offered as part of this retreat will close with a Thought, Word, and Deed section. A few prompts or questions will be offered to help you note your thoughts in response to what you have just read. You might want to write down your thoughts in a journal to help you clarify them. There will also be a few prompts and questions to help you decide if you want to have a word, or a conversation, with someone about what you have just read. Finally, you will be invited to reflect on whether you are being called to do something different—a deed, in response to what you have read. There is a saying from the twelve-step movement that we have to "do different, to get different." This "doing different" could be in thought, word, or deed. The intention of this retreat is to help you to reflect on your thoughts, words, and deeds, your current way of doing things, and perhaps for you to begin to "do different, to get different."

You can do all of this reflection on your thoughts, words, and deeds in a journal. If you are doing the retreat with others, then you will be invited to share your reflections with them. There is a wonderful experience of support and accountability when we share our thoughts, words, and deeds with others; I encourage you to look for opportunities to share your experiences with others, even if you are not participating in this retreat as part of a group.

Many churches use a prayer of confession in their corporate worship that includes the phrase "thought, word, and deed." In the Episcopal Church, for example, the congregation prays to God, "We have sinned against you in thought, word, and deed, by what we have done, and by what we have left undone." While praying this prayer people may take a look back in time at their recent thoughts, words, and deeds and express regret for how they have fallen short of what God intended for them and then promise to go forward with good intentions.

On this retreat you will have the opportunity to look forward regarding your own thoughts, words, and deeds. You will be encouraged to be proactive about creating thoughts, words, and deeds that will more fully align with your spiritual beliefs and values and enhance your wellness, as well as the wellness of your family and your surrounding community. While I believe that looking back and confessing our shortcomings can be a healthy thing to do, I strongly believe that looking forward by focusing and strengthening our intentions to live well is equally important.

Suggestions for How to Use This Book

The core of this book is the self-guided retreat found in chapters two through nine, while the first chapter serves as preparation for the retreat and the final chapter is for reflection on your experience of the retreat. The first chapter presents the foundational thinking upon which the retreat is based. Whenever we are going on an important journey, we are likely to spend time preparing for that journey, and this journey is no different. Reading the first chapter will help you prepare for this retreat and will maximize your chances of getting the most out of it.

Chapter ten, the final chapter, provides thoughts on how to continue to carry what you have learned from your retreat into your life. Remember that being well is not an end in and of itself. Our own wellness, or lack of wellness, has an impact on the world around us. The more well we are, the more positive an impact we can have in the world. If we are well our families will be healthier and happier, and so will the communities in which we live. We can make a difference in what our world looks and feels like.

Chapter ten will discuss ideas of how we can be instruments of peace and wellness for others.

The retreat in this book can be done privately or it can be done with others. Most people report that they get greater benefit from this kind of retreat when they do it with others but that is up to you. You might do it with a friend, a loved one, or in a small group or class at your church or within your faith community. Participating in a retreat with others is fun and we can benefit from the wisdom of others as well as from the built-in accountability that comes from being in a group.

If you don't already have a journal, I recommend that you purchase one to use in conjunction with this book. Throughout your retreat you will be invited to note your thoughts and responses to the reflections. You will also be asked to reflect on a word or a conversation you might wish to have with someone based on insights you have gained. Finally, you will be asked to reflect on any deeds you feel inspired to do in response to the thoughts and words that you have had. A journal is an ideal way to record your thoughts, words, and deeds as you proceed with your retreat.

Each segment of your retreat begins with the part of the Living Compass self-assessment that corresponds to that area of wellness. The complete set of Living Compass self-assessment forms can found in the appendix of this book. To complete this self-assessment you will scale yourself on eighty statements and then shade in your results on the Living Compass Self-Assessment Tool in the appendix. The self-assessments are also provided in the online resource that Church Publishing has created and that is available at www.churchpublishing.org/yourlivingcompass. The resource provides the self-assessments in each of the eight areas of wellness that this retreat addresses. You can download and print this free resource for your personal use. The self-assessments are also available on the Living Compass website, and on our Living Well With Living Compass App. You may prefer using one of those options if you do not want to write on the pages of this book. You are also welcome to photocopy the self-assessment pages for your own personal use.

There are a total of forty reflections in the self-guided retreat. If you read one per day, you would complete the retreat in just under six weeks. If you read one reflection per week, you would complete the retreat in nine months. This might be an ideal pace for a group that meets weekly to discuss the reflections. Or you can set your own pace and move on to the next reflection when you feel ready. Interruptions in life are inevitable. Don't worry if this happens. Just pick up where you left off. Reading the reflections in a specific order is not important, either. Feel free to do them in any order that suits you and your life. Let the Spirit guide you.

Just as it is a good idea to get an annual physical, I recommend that you think of this retreat as your annual whole-person wellness check-up and consider doing it once a year. While the readings will be the same if you do the retreat again, your life will not be the same and you will get something different from the readings. Each time you go through this self-guided retreat, your thoughts, words, and deeds will be different.

In the end, there is no "right" way to use this book. Let the Spirit guide you toward the most beneficial way to use this resource. Be patient with yourself and with the process, and in the end you cannot help but be changed by the work you will have done.

The Quakers have a wonderful saying that they use when they pray for someone. They say, "I will hold you in the Light." Know that I will be holding you collectively in the Light as you head out on your journey of wholeness and wellness.

Chapter 1

PREPARING FOR YOUR RETREAT

Put Your Whole Self In

Children's songs are some of my favorite music. There is a simplicity and silliness to many children's songs that makes them infectious; familiar children's songs jump easily into our heads. Just reading the words, "If you're happy and you know it," probably has you singing in your head right now.

The children's song "The Hokey Pokey" has always been my favorite. I play the guitar and love to sing for both children and elders. Both groups seem to love to sing and get up and move whenever they hear the song. Of course you don't just sing "The Hokey Pokey," you *do* the Hokey Pokey. This combination of singing and moving is probably why this song is so memorable.

"The Hokey Pokey" begins by inviting you to "put your right hand in," and then to take it out, put it back in, and shake it all about. After that you do the Hokey Pokey and you turn yourself about. The song progresses from there by inviting you to put your left hand in, then your right and left legs, then your head, and the favorite verse for children—your "backside"!

"The Hokey Pokey" builds toward the last verse when you are asked to "put your whole self in." I share all of this with you because much like the Hokey Pokey, this retreat is an invitation to put your whole self in. You will reflect upon your wellness with all your heart, all your soul, all your strength, and all your mind. Eight areas of your life and wellness will be examined, one in each chapter: Spirituality, Rest and Play, Vocational Wellness, Organization, Care for the Body, Stress Resiliency, Relationships, and Handling Your Emotions. When you have concluded this retreat you will have reflected upon all aspects of your health and wellness and in your own way you will have done the Hokey Pokey—you will have put your whole self in.

Have you seen the bumper sticker that reads, "What If the Hokey Pokey Is What It's All About?" I am pretty sure that the Hokey Pokey is *not* what it's all about, but when it comes to caring for your health and wellness, I am very sure that putting your whole self in *is*. My hope is that this book will be a place to help you determine the best course of action for treating any discomforts you may be experiencing and to become inspired to turn your life, your relationships, your work, and your health and wellness around.

Looking For Your Balance

One fall Saturday when our son was three I was painting the front porch of our old house with his help. At one point I was standing on a short step ladder and while leaning over to paint the soffit of the porch, I lost my balance and fell into the bushes five feet below. I wasn't hurt, but it shook me up for a few moments and I lay dazed in the bushes. Our son was quite alarmed and ran down to ask me what happened. After catching my breath I explained to him that I was fine and that I had simply lost my balance. A few minutes later, after returning to my painting, I noticed our son crawling around on his hands and knees looking under the bushes by the porch. When I asked him what he was doing, he innocently replied, "Daddy, I'm looking for your balance." Laughing to myself, I realized what he thought I meant by losing my balance: it only made sense that he would try to find it for me. If I had told him I had lost my screwdriver, he would have no doubt looked for that as well. So why would he not look for my balance? I bet we all wish it were that simple—that whenever we lose our balance in life someone else, even a three year old, could find it and give it back to us.

Unfortunately others cannot find our balance for us. However, the good news is that whenever we discover that we have lost our balance, we can take steps to regain it. Perhaps you are reading this book because you are looking for a way to restore balance and wellness to your life. Perhaps you are looking to restore balance and wellness to a significant relationship in your life, to your financial life, or to your work life. Perhaps you are struggling with a health issue or experiencing an unhealthy amount of stress in your life. If you are experiencing any or all of these challenges to maintaining balance and wellness, do not feel embarrassed or critical of yourself; instead, understand that you are part of the human race and it is a part of being an imperfect human being. You are not alone. The fact that you are reading this book probably means you want to do something proactive for yourself, and you are trying to find your balance. I am hoping that reading and working the process in this book will be a great step in that direction.

Your Faith *Can* Make You Well

There are many outstanding wellness programs today, but few of them invite people to explore the vital connection between their spirituality and their current state of wellness. Up until very recently, most wellness programs focused primarily on the physical dimension of wellness. There is now, however, a renewed interest in not only addressing spirituality as it relates to one's wellness, but to looking at other dimensions of wellness, too. This approach to wellness, known as "whole-person wellness," is what this book is based upon. In this book we address what it means to be well with all your heart, with all your soul, with all your strength, and with all your mind. These four categories of wellness comprise the four points of the Living Compass approach to health and wellness.

In the Bible there is a story about health and wellness that appears in the fifth chapter of the Gospel of John. In this story we learn of a man sitting by a pool in Jerusalem and hoping to be healed as he encounters Jesus. The story says that there were many blind, lame, and paralyzed people there seeking healing. The gospel tells us that the man we come to know in the story has been ill for thirty-eight years. When Jesus approaches this desperate man, he asks him a fascinating question: "Do you want to be made well?"

This question seems rather silly at first. Of course a person who has been ill for thirty-eight years wants to be well, right? And yet, if we pause to consider this question we will discover that when it comes to wellness, it is *the* question. We all know people who seem to choose to stay stuck in their "dis-ease." They seem to be blind, lame, or paralyzed about their ability to make a choice to be well. We, of course, are sometimes those people ourselves. Any of us can be blind, lame, or paralyzed regarding our own well-being or the well-being of a significant relationship without even realizing it. We can be blind to the steps we could take to be made well. Like the man that Jesus encountered by the healing pool in Jerusalem, sometimes we need someone outside of ourselves to help us recognize both our present condition and what we can do to change it. Sometimes that someone is another person and sometimes it's the work of the Spirit, and of course, sometimes it's one and the same. The connection between the Spirit and wellness is evident in many of the stories that describe Jesus offering healing to someone. The stories almost always end with Jesus saying to the person, "Your faith has made you well."

It is reported that Mark Twain, when asked if he believed in infant baptism, said, "Believe in it? Heck, I've seen it!" That is funny but is also exactly my response when I am asked if I believe there is connection between faith and wellness: "Believe it? Heck, I've seen it!" It is because I have witnessed the connection between faith and the healing, recovery, and well-being of countless peoples' lives that I continuously emphasize the importance of grounding one's wellness in one's faith. The fruits of wellness truly grow from nurturing the seeds of the Spirit's movement in one's life.

It is worth noting here that the power of faith in a person's life can work two ways. I have been speaking of the tremendous positive influence a faith or spiritual life can have on a person's health and wellness. The fact is the power of a person's faith system or spiritual understandings can also have a tremendous negative influence on a person's health and wellness. In my thirty plus years as a psychotherapist, I have listened to hundreds of individuals describe how they were suffering from having been raised in what I call a toxic faith environment. A toxic faith environment is characterized by a shame-based or fear-based approach to spirituality. The approach of toxic faith is to shame and/or scare people into believing and behaving a certain way. Not only does this not work in the long term, but it creates residual shame, anxiety, and inadequacy in a person. In this case, I would say that rather than their faith making them well, their faith has actually helped to make them sick.

You Have Already Been Made Whole

Our wholeness is a gift that we have already been given by God. We already are whole. But sometimes we can get a bit off balance and may not be experiencing this God-given gift, and therefore are feeling unwell. I use the words "wholeness" and "wellness" in slightly different ways. Wholeness has to do with our being, the very essence of who we are. Wellness has to do with how we are choosing or not choosing to manifest that wholeness at any given time. Wellness is the sum total of our choices. Wholeness is the sum total of God's choice to create and love us. We have already been given the gift of wholeness.

The retreat you are about to embark on is meant to help you discover a deeper sense of wholeness and to create wellness choices that more fully manifest that wholeness in your life. It is also meant to help you identify places where healing is needed in your life. Healing begins the moment we begin to recognize the gift of wholeness, the gift of love that has already been freely given to us. And the more we recognize that gift, the more likely we are to manifest it in our own wellness.

It is my hope and prayer that this retreat will help you to recognize and receive the gift of wholeness that you have already been given and in the process help you to share that gift more freely with others.

Your Living Compass

We all have places that are sacred to us, places where we reconnect to our sense of what is most important in life. These sacred places are where we experience that which is holy, that which is life-giving. Sacred places help us access a different place within ourselves.

Quetico Provincial Park in western Ontario is one of the sacred places in my life. Quetico is a 1.2 million acre remote wilderness area that borders the Boundary Waters Canoe Area in northern Minnesota, and like the Boundary Waters it can only be accessed by canoe. A permit is required to enter the park, which limits the number of people in the park at any one time. It is common to go several days without seeing another soul. I have spent many days and nights in this park and have always drunk the water right out of the lake. No filtering, boiling, or treatment of the water is required. If you relish solitude in nature, the experience there is as pure as the water.

There is one essential skill for a successful canoe journey through any remote wilderness and that is the skill of navigation. One must be proficient in using a compass and reading a map. There are more than six hundred lakes in Quetico and, depending on how long one's journey, a visit may include ten to fifteen of those lakes in a week. The portage trails are remote and are never marked so they can only be found by using a compass and a good map. No one would ever think of entering a remote wilderness area without a good compass and a good map.

The reality is that each of us already has a "living" compass. Each of us has a compass that is directing and guiding the day-to-day decisions we make in our lives, whether we know it or not. Our compass is a combination of our beliefs, thoughts, core values, self-identity, passions, and ideals and is always orienting our lives and our daily decisions.

There are many compasses that are competing to guide how we make decisions, including our family of origin, our gender, our race, our national culture, our important relationships, our self-identity, and our faith. These compasses all influence our daily decisions, often without us even knowing it.

This retreat invites you to reflect on the compass or compasses that are orienting you in eight areas of wellness. In each of these areas you will be invited to reflect on which compass is guiding the choices and decisions you make regarding this area of wellness. You will be invited to reflect on what thoughts, beliefs, ideals, passions, and ideals are influencing your decisions.

Throughout the retreat you will be invited to take your reflections a couple of steps further. After you reflect on thoughts, beliefs, passions, and ideals that are guiding your decisions, you will be asked to consider the impact on your well-being. Are you helped or hurt by those thoughts, beliefs, passions, and ideals? Finally, you will be invited to decide if you want to do or try something different based on your self-reflection. The following three questions provide a simple way to summarize this:

◆ What compass or compasses are guiding you in this area of wellness?

◆ If you keep heading in the direction you are pointed, will you end up where you want to be?

◆ Is there anything you would like to change or do differently based on your answers to the first two questions?

Faith Defined as Your Inner Compass

There are many different ways to define faith. For the purposes of this retreat, I am defining faith as the composite of one's thoughts, beliefs, passions, practices, habits, and ideals that serve as the inner compass that guides one's life. Every one of us has an inner, living compass—and probably more than one—that guides us, whether we are conscious of it or not. It is probably clear by now that I view spirituality as the area of wellness that influences and guides the remaining seven areas of wellness identified by the Living Compass. It is the foundation upon which we build our lives and make our decisions and is the most important part of who we are.

The idea of a compass works well as a metaphor for our faith. While it is common to talk about the needle of a compass pointing north, in fact, the needle is not really pointing, but is actually being pulled toward the north. The needle of a compass is activated and influenced by a force outside of itself. This force, known as magnetic north, is what causes the needle of a compass to point toward the north. Our faith works the same way. Our spiritual life is activated and influenced by a force outside of ourselves. Christians, of course, name this force as God/Jesus/Spirit, while other traditions give different names to that which is drawing us toward the true north of an abundant and meaningful life.

Change Your Compass, Change Your Life

There are a host of wellness programs available to us today. Wellness programs are popular in workplaces, schools, retirement communities, hospitals, and through many health insurance companies. All of these wellness programs have something important and helpful to offer. They all provide good information about disease prevention and positive changes with the potential to increase health and wellness. Behavior change is a primary focus of most wellness programs. The Living Compass approach to wellness is a little different from most of these wellness programs. The goal of our approach to wellness is to make our faith our living compass every day, in every way, in every aspect of our lives. Of course new behaviors and habits will follow from this transformation of consciousness, but if we just focus on changing behaviors without changing consciousness, then our behavior changes will most likely be short lived.

Two Prayers to Guide Us as We Begin Our Retreat

As our final preparation for beginning our retreat, I invite you pray two ancient prayers. I invite you to pray them now and to return to them and pray them throughout your retreat. The first prayer is the prayer attributed to St. Francis.

> Lord, make us instruments of your peace. Where there is hatred, let us sow love; where there is injury, pardon; where there is discord, union; where there is doubt, faith; where there is despair, hope; where there is darkness, light; where there is sadness, joy. Grant that we may not so much seek to be consoled as to console; to be understood as to understand; to be loved as to love. For it is in giving that we receive; it is in pardoning that we are pardoned; and it is in dying that we are born to eternal life. Amen. (BCP, 833)

This prayer is a beautiful summary of what it means to live a Christian life. If we think of being an instrument in musical terms, then it is essential that we tune our instruments on a regular basis. If we are out of tune, it's impossible to play beautiful music. This retreat is designed to help you tune the instrument of your heart, soul, strength, and mind so that you can truly be an instrument of God's healing love in the world.

The second prayer I would like to invite you to pray is the Collect for Purity.

> Almighty God, to you all hearts are open, all desires known, and from you no secrets are hid: Cleanse the thoughts of our hearts by the inspiration of your Holy Spirit, that we may perfectly love you, and worthily magnify your holy Name; through Christ our Lord. Amen. (BCP, 355)

A full reflection on this prayer will be offered later in this retreat. I include it here, too, because just as it is an ideal prayer to begin worship, it is an ideal prayer for beginning a retreat. This prayer, just as the retreat that follows, invites us to authenticity and full transparency in order that we may grow in our ability to love and magnify God's presence in our lives and in the world.

So let's begin. Let's open our hearts more fully to ourselves, to one another, and to God.

Living Well With All Your
SOUL

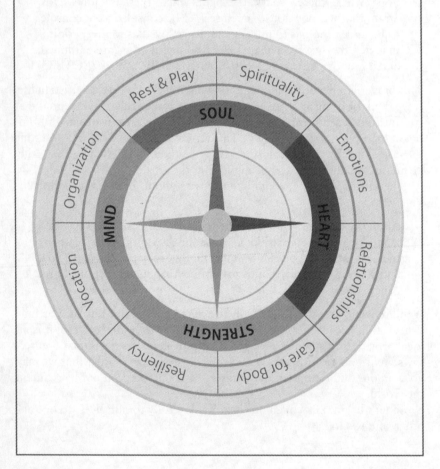

Chapter 2

SPIRITUALITY

Reflection 1

Assessing Your Spiritual Wellness

As you begin your reflection on each of the eight areas of wellness, you will start with a self-assessment. If you have ever used navigational software on either a smartphone or in a car, you know that the software will always give directions from your "current location." The Living Compass Self-Assessment Tool helps you determine your "current location" in each of the eight areas of wellness that this retreat addresses. The self-assessment is a snapshot of your state of wellness and balance at the moment you take it. It identifies how you are living and feeling currently. It identifies a starting place for you. In fact, as you will see, this entire retreat is an ongoing process of self-assessment and self-reflection. The very fact that you are committed to engaging in this process of assessment and reflection is in and of itself the most important factor influencing your personal growth and wellness. It means that you are willing to look at your life honestly and to think seriously about how you can let God be your compass in the day-to-day living of your life.

I invite you to complete the Spirituality self-assessment now, using the form provided in the appendix of this book, writing the responses in your journal, or printing the online version on a separate piece of paper. When you are finished, transfer your number to the Spirituality wedge of the compass tool on page 155.

Private and Communal Dimensions
There are a couple of important insights regarding spirituality that are reflected in the statements of this self-assessment. The first is that spirituality has both private and communal dimensions. There are things that we do on our own to nurture and strengthen our spirituality and there are things

that we do in community with others to both express and strengthen our spirituality.

I have found that for many people one of these two dimensions of spirituality comes more naturally than the other. Some people are more comfortable with spirituality as a private matter, nourishing their spiritual life with a private prayer life and by reading spiritual books or walking in nature, but they do not have a faith community that they feel comfortable participating in. Others are active in their church or faith community, but do not have any kind of daily or regular practices to feed their spirituality. For these people it's as if active participation in and through a faith community is how they express and practice their spirituality, rarely feeling the need for something private to nourish their spirituality.

I invite you to reflect upon how comfortable you are in practicing both the public and private dimensions of your spirituality. If one of the two dimensions of spirituality is less comfortable for you, I invite you to pay more attention to that aspect of your spirituality. If you feel uncomfortable finding a church or faith community to participate in, yet you think it might enrich your spiritual life, I invite you to move out of your comfort zone and experiment with visiting some churches. If you know someone who actively participates in a church, you might want to ask about her church and inquire if you could attend with her sometime. And if you feel uncomfortable with developing the private dimension of your spirituality, yet you think it might enrich your spiritual life, I invite you to move out of your comfort zone and experiment with a daily practice of prayer, meditation, or spiritual reading. As you will find with all areas of wellness, growth most often occurs when we are willing to try something new and different.

Spirituality, like most everything else in life, can be practiced. A vital spirituality is not just something that some people happen to have and some people do not, anymore than a healthy relationship is something that some people happen to have and some people do not. Spirituality, like a healthy relationship, is something that is created and maintained through regular practice.

A spiritual practice is anything you do to intentionally nourish and strengthen your soul and your connection with the Divine. Common spiritual practices are prayer, meditation, spiritual reading, worship, involvement in a faith community, doing service, and going on a retreat. But, because each person and each soul is unique, what nourishes your soul is as unique as you are. I have also found that over time I need to vary the practices that feed my soul. Just as I like to change my physical workout habits from time to time, I find that changing my "spiritual workout" habits is helpful for keeping them fresh, lively, and meaningful.

I saw quite often when I served as a pastor of a church that people needed different kinds of experiences to nurture their spiritual life during different times of their lives. It was common for new people joining the church to tell me that they had not been a part of a church for a long time—

or perhaps ever—but they just felt that at the particular stage of life they were in now it was important for them to be part of a faith community. They recognized what their soul needed and took action to meet that need. Perhaps there was a time in your life when the thought of going on a retreat or working with a spiritual director never occurred to you, but now you find yourself considering such things.

Spiritual practices are so important that I recommend you make a concerted effort to maintain at least one spiritual practice throughout the duration of this retreat. Spirituality is the soil within which all of the areas of wellness take root and grow. Keeping your spiritual soil healthy will assist you in whatever other aspects of wellness you choose to nurture and grow, throughout this self-guided retreat and beyond.

▶ Thought

What thoughts or feelings did the Spirituality self-assessment bring up for you?

What do you think of the idea that spirituality has both a private and a communal dimension? Do you recognize the need for both of these dimensions in your own life?

▶ Word

Are you comfortable talking about your spirituality with others?

Do you know people who are comfortable talking about their spirituality, and would you be willing to ask them about how they practice and nourish their spiritual life?

▶ Deed

Based on the results of your Spirituality self-assessment, is there anything different you want to do related to your spiritual wellness?

Do you currently do anything on a regular basis that you consider to be a spiritual practice?

Would you consider trying a new spiritual practice that might initially feel uncomfortable?

Reflection 2

What Makes Your Face Shine?

When you or I tell a story about something that is truly life-giving for us, those listening will almost always notice something as we tell the story.

Our whole face lights up. We have all had that experience of witnessing this in others. We cannot help but reflect it when we are connecting our hearts, souls, and words to that which gives us such delight.

In my work as a psychotherapist, spiritual director, and Episcopal priest, I often ask people to tell me a story about a recent experience of great joy and delight. Every time a person recounts such a story, his or her face lights up. In fact, one way we can be sure that we are connecting with the Spirit in our lives is to notice when our whole energy shifts. When our energy shifts there will always be some kind of physical manifestation of that joy and delight. We can feel it and others will notice it.

There is a story written some three thousand years ago that describes this phenomenon. The story is found in the Bible, in the book of Exodus. In this story, Moses has just come down from the top of Mount Sinai where he has been connecting with God and in the process receives the two tablets, the Ten Commandments, of the covenant from God. The story says that "as he came down from the mountain with the two tablets of the covenant in his hand, Moses did not know that the skin of his face shone because he had been walking with God" (Exodus 34:29). The story goes on to add that when others saw Moses, "the skin of his face was shining, and they were afraid to come near him" (Exodus 34:30).

I love this story! I think part of why I love it is that it is so easy for me to picture Moses and his shining face. It is easy to picture this happening because while it is a story of connecting with God, it is also a very human story. Just the other day a friend of mine who has been saddened by the ending of a significant relationship was telling me that she has met someone new and she thinks that she might be falling in love again. As she told me this story her face was shining. And not just her face, but her whole body was radiating joy. In fact, as she was telling the story she was moving and swaying her body around. She was so full of life and energy that she literally could not stand still.

So one thing that causes our faces to shine is to do what Moses did: connect with God. We don't have to go up to the top of a mountain to connect with God (although for many people this is a true spiritual experience) and to experience what Moses felt. A vital, love-based spirituality that is nurtured and cared for will indeed manifest itself as joy and wellness in our lives, and our whole selves will shine.

In my experience the opposite can occur as well. We have all had the experience of looking into someone's face, sensing immediately that there is something wrong. When a person is scared, angry, sad, or insecure, her face will reveal this, too.

For every person I have known experiencing a life-giving, shine-producing experience of spirituality and God, I have known someone who is experiencing just the opposite. For these people, their experience of God and/or religion has been something negative. Their experience of God and/or religion has most likely been grounded in shame, fear, and/or guilt.

When I meet with someone for spiritual direction it is easy to discern whether their experience with religion has been love-based or shame-based. This difference applies, too, to how a person was parented. Love-based parenting and shame-based parenting create two very different feelings in a child, just as love-based faith and shame-based faith produce two very different feelings in an adult.

Obeying God out of fear and guilt is a hallmark of shame-based spirituality. Longing to connect with God out of a desire to be well and to be revitalized is a hallmark of love-based spirituality. When I talk about love-based spirituality, please know that I do not for a moment discount the importance of moral and ethical behavior, or the importance of feeling appropriate guilt when one has done wrong. There is a big difference between feeling appropriate guilt and being bound by shame. It has been said that guilt is related to something you have done, and that shame is a feeling of something you are—it has to do with your very being. A loving God would not want anyone to live in shame.

Remember the quotation from Irenaeus, who wrote that "the glory of God is a human being fully alive"? For our purposes, I would like to suggest a slight adaptation: "To ground one's spirituality in a loving experience of God is to make one's face shine and to feel fully alive."

▶ Thought

Think or write down some thoughts about times when your face has shone. What thoughts, experiences, and/or people were associated with those times?

Looking back on your upbringing, were you raised with a love-based spirituality, a shame-based spirituality, or not much sense of spirituality at all? How has that affected your relationship with God?

▶ Word

What kind of conversations help you to feel vital and alive, connected with your spiritual self? What is different about these kinds of conversations and how might you have more of them?

Is there anyone with whom you would like to talk regarding what you have experienced from reading this reflection?

▶ Deed

What activities help you to feel the sense of delight and of being fully alive just described?

What new experiences might you like to start doing to more fully enhance and or express your spirituality?

Reflection 3

Spirituality: The Root System That Grounds Our Wellness

One of my favorite stories in the Bible is a teaching story that Jesus shared with his followers known as the Parable of the Sower. I share the story with you here because I believe it has so much to teach us about spirituality.

> That same day Jesus went out of the house and sat beside the sea. Such great crowds gathered around him that he got into a boat and sat there, while the whole crowd stood on the beach. And he told them many things in parables, saying: "Listen! A sower went out to sow. And as he sowed, some seeds fell on the path, and the birds came and ate them up. Other seeds fell on rocky ground, where they did not have much soil, and they sprang up quickly, since they had no depth of soil. But when the sun rose, they were scorched; and since they had no root, they withered away. Other seeds fell among thorns, and the thorns grew up and choked them. Other seeds fell on good soil and brought forth grain, some a hundredfold, some sixty, some thirty. Let anyone with ears listen!" (Matthew 13:1–9)

In some ways I think the parable is misnamed. A more descriptive name might be the "Parable of the Soil" because it really is a story about the soil more than it is about the sower. The sower and the seeds are the same in each scenario. What is different is the soil on which the seeds fall. The seeds that fall on the hardened path do not have much of a chance of taking root. The seeds that fall on the rocky and thorny soil grow for a short time, but are not able to sustain their growth. Only the seeds that fall on the good soil can take root and grow, returning a great harvest in the process.

A literal interpretation of this parable is that in order for a plant or tree to grow stronger and taller, it must first develop a deeper root system to support its growth. Without a deep root system, the plant or tree will topple over, especially in the midst of threatening or challenging conditions.

I think the same is true for human beings; we need rich soil and a strong root system to help us stand tall in the midst of any storms that come in to our lives. That rich soil and strong root system is our spirituality. The Parable of the Sower reminds us that the most important ingredient in growing a strong root system of any type is to have deep, rich soil. Rocks and thorns in our soil make it hard for us to support growth in our lives. Proof of this is offered to us every day when we read of a public person, whether it be a celebrity, politician, musician, or sports figure, whose ascent to quick fame is matched by an equal and opposite descent due to some kind of crisis, an indication that they were not well grounded. Without a strong spiritual root system, any of us can easily topple.

When it comes to wellness, there is direct application of the wisdom of this parable. Our spirituality is the soil within which the roots of our wellness are grounded. This includes our emotional, relational, physical, financial, vocational, and intellectual wellness. The wisdom of this parable is that in order to create new growth in our lives, we first need to be sure that our soil can sustain and nurture the roots that will be necessary for this growth.

This is the perspective that is missing in many wellness programs. Many wellness programs focus primarily on making lifestyle and behavior changes. Healthy habits are taught and motivation is offered to break unhealthy habits. This is all well and good as far as it goes. However, I know for myself that when I try to make positive changes without first experiencing a change of heart and/or a change of consciousness, those changes are usually short-lived. Those kinds of changes spring up quickly, but soon wither away. I call these kinds of changes "outside, in" changes, because the impetus for the change is coming more from outside ourselves rather than from within.

If, however, our desire to change is rooted in and grows out of our spirituality, there is a greater chance that the changes will last. This is because these changes are coming from the "inside, out." "Inside, out" changes emerge from a change in heart and/or a change of consciousness. Another way to think about why our spirituality is so fundamental to guiding us in all the other areas of wellness is to remember the image of our spirituality as our inner compass; it guides our daily decisions and choices.

Thinking of our spirituality as our inner compass reminds us that it can direct and guide every aspect of our lives. For example, our spirituality and the values that accompany it not only give us guidance regarding how to create loving and just relationships with our neighbors, they also remind us that it is essential that we do so. Our spirituality not only provides guidance regarding how we are to relate to money and material wealth, it also clearly warns us of the dangers of not getting those relationships right.

As a priest I have had the honor of being with many people in the final months, weeks, days, and moments of their lives. To walk this journey with someone who is dying is a sacred privilege. What I have found to be true in these experiences is that as all the other dimensions of a person's life are constricting and coming to an end, what remains is a person's spirituality. In fact, I have often had the experience of seeing someone's spirituality expand and blossom in their final days or weeks. It has not been uncommon in my experience to see someone's face and spirit shine, even as they are dying. Such is the power of a deeply rooted spirituality.

▶ Thought

What are your thoughts as you read this reflection? What speaks
to your spirit? Does it ring true for you and fit with your way
of thinking about spirituality?

Do you have any thoughts about any "rocks" or "thorns" that are
present in the soil of your life right now that might make it
challenging to deepen your spiritual wellness?

▶ Word

Is there a word or a conversation you would like to have with
someone about your spirituality? Who might that be? Are you
willing to have that conversation?

Language is very important when it comes to both experiencing
and expressing our spirituality. For some people, traditional
religious language inspires and feeds their spirituality, while for
others, traditional religious language has the opposite effect. Is
there any particular religious language that inspires you? Is
there any religious language that is off-putting for you?

▶ Deed

What specific actions and/or activities help you nurture and
express your spirituality?

Is there anything you wish to try or do differently to help free your
soil from any rocks and thorns that could be impeding the
growth of your spiritual life?

Reflection 4

Receive, Release: A Simple Spiritual Practice

We know that in order to become proficient at anything worthwhile that
we will have to practice. If we want to develop the ability to play the piano,
guitar, or any other musical instrument, we will need to practice. If we
want learn to sing, knit, or learn to speak a new language, we will need to
practice. If we want to improve our ability to hit a baseball, a golf ball, or
a tennis ball, we will need to practice.

This same truth applies to our spirituality. If we want to develop, grow,
or improve our spiritual life, we will need to practice. The idea of practicing
your spirituality may be new to you, but spiritual practices have been

around for thousands of years and they are an essential part of every religion. Prayer, for instance, both its private and communal expressions, is a spiritual practice.

Everyone can benefit from a spiritual practice. A spiritual practice is simply a way of consciously connecting with God. There is no "right" spiritual practice; everyone must find what is right for them. Singing, walking, praying, journaling, meditating, cooking, conversing, serving, forgiving, writing, creating, gardening, running, kayaking, biking, making music, worshipping, drawing, and dancing can all be spiritual practices.

When it comes to connecting spirituality and wellness, I have one spiritual practice that works especially well. Everyone I know who has developed this practice has reported positive benefits. This practice that works so well is known as centering prayer.

The focus of centering prayer is conscious contact with God. There is a beautiful description of centering prayer as "resting in God." When a person has practiced centering prayer for a while, it is common for them to experience a true sense of resting in God. If you think of our conscious mind and its constant thoughts as the surface of a large body of water, then the goal of centering prayer is to get us to a deeper place within our souls, down beneath the bouncing waves of our chattering thoughts. With both the ocean and our souls, when we dive deeper we find stillness. In the language of the previous reflection, think of distracting or negative thoughts as rocks and thorns. Centering prayer helps us remove some of those rocks and thorns in order to enrich the soil of our souls and to allow for more stillness within

"Be still, and know that I am God," says Psalm 46. Most us would love to be able to be more still and experience God's presence, but are unsure how to do that. Just thinking about being still doesn't make it happen. In fact, if we are honest, most of us find that the harder we try to think about being still the more churned up we become. Centering prayer is a concrete way to practice being still and experiencing God's quiet presence.

Because our minds are prone to wander and bounce around like the waves on the surface of the ocean when we are trying to be still, the practice of centering prayer advises us to choose a word or phrase that we can return to over and over again whenever our minds begin to wander. Returning to this word or phrase will help settle our minds and allow us to go deeper in to the still place within our souls.

Practicing Receive, Release
When I lead retreats I frequently lead the group in this very simple centering prayer practice, and I invite you to try it here. I recommend that you read the full instructions first, and then try the practice on your own.

First, find a comfortable sitting position, place your hands on your lap with your palms up, and close your eyes.

Next, begin to take moderately deep breaths and gradually slow down your breathing. Continue this slower breathing for a short time, then begin to repeat the word "receive" silently in your mind each time you inhale. After a short time, begin to repeat the word "release" each time you exhale. So it's "receive" as you inhale, and "release" as you exhale. These two words will help focus your mind whenever it begins to wander.

As you repeat the word "receive" imagine yourself receiving exactly what God wants to give to you right now. As you repeat the word "release" imagine yourself releasing to God what it is you need to let go of at this time. Start out by doing this practice for three to five minutes. It is helpful to set a timer. As you feel more comfortable with this practice you can extend the time. (Several meditation timer apps exist for smartphones.)

This version of "receive, release" works well on its own and you may want to leave it at that, but you may want to add one other aspect to this practice that is particularly helpful when you are experiencing worry or stress.

After you have closed your eyes and have slowed down your breathing, but before you begin repeating "receive, release" in your mind, bring the stressful or worrisome concern to mind. It might be a health concern, a relationship concern, a financial concern, or just a general sense of worry or stress.

Begin the mindful repetition of "receive, release" and imagine what it is you need to receive from God to help you with this stress or worry, and what it is you need to release to God to help lighten the burden this stress or worry is causing you. You may even find that God gives you a word or phrase to use in place of "receive" or "release." You might, for example, find yourself mindfully repeating "patience," "kindness," or "forgiveness" on your in-breath and perhaps something like "control," "anger," "judgment" on the out-breath.

This practice can be done anytime, anywhere. The beauty of this simple practice is that if you do it with your eyes open no one will know that you are doing it. If you are losing your calm in a meeting, you can do it. You can also do it if you are waiting in line or are stuck in traffic. I find that it is very helpful to do this mindfulness practice as preparation for a high stress meeting or situation. When I do that I find that I enter that meeting or situation with greater calmness and greater clarity. Many people have reported to me that they find this practice is helpful when they are having trouble sleeping.

There are dozens of books written about centering prayer and meditation and the similarities and differences between the two. I encourage you to read on your own if you want to learn more about these ancient practices. They have worked for millions of people over the ages.

Whether you try this particular spiritual practice or not, I truly hope you will find a spiritual practice that works for you and that you stick with it. It will be worth your time and effort, and I am confident you will notice a positive effect on other areas of your wellness.

▶ Thought

What thoughts do you have about the idea of developing a spiritual practice?

This reflection states that our thoughts can distract us and get in the way of our ability to connect with God. Is this true in your experience? If so, how? What helps calm your thoughts when you are worried or stressed?

▶ Word

Do you know someone who has experience with spiritual practices that are different from yours or seem outside your "comfort zone"? Would you be willing to have a conversation with that person to learn from his or her experience?

Are there particular words that you use when you pray? Are these words you have memorized, or do you read them from a book or other resource? Do you know any prayers by memory? Might you want to learn one?

▶ Deed

This reflection lists many everyday activities that can become spiritual practices. Have you ever done, or do you currently do, an everyday activity in a way that it is a spiritual practice for you?

Are you willing to try the "receive, release" centering prayer practice? If not, what else could you try instead?

Reflection 5

Pay Attention to What You Pay Attention To

The fact that you are working your way through this retreat is evidence that you have made a commitment to pay closer attention to your well-being. More specifically, you have made a decision to pay more attention to the connection between your spirituality and other areas of wellness in your life. In each of these areas of wellness you are paying closer attention to your thoughts, words, and deeds and how each of these shape and influence your well-being.

The act of paying attention is so simple and yet, so very important. It is so important that I remind myself and others to "pay attention to what you pay attention to." This little piece of wisdom has much to do with our spirituality because our spirituality directs and shapes *what* we pay attention to and *how* we pay attention.

Jesus created scandal for many people because he paid attention to people who were shunned by his society and seen as outcasts. And the scandal wasn't just *that* he chose to pay attention to the poor, lepers, prostitutes, Samaritans, and tax collectors, but also *how* he paid attention to them. He paid loving attention to them, offering them healing and calling society to address the issues of injustice and prejudice that caused them to be shunned. What Jesus was doing was in stark contrast to the kind of attention that other religious authorities were paying to these same people. The attention that other religious authorities were paying to these marginalized people was filled with judgment and contempt. Jesus modeled a different way of paying attention, a trait common to all great spiritual leaders. He loved them.

Being present to and paying attention to those people who are marginalized in our world is an essential part of deepening our spirituality. Having a mature spirituality means that we pay attention to people who are poor, lonely, sick, disabled, aged, or victims of prejudice, violence, and injustice. Just as importantly it means that our attention leads to actions that care for the people who are marginalized. It all starts with attention, though. We cannot act with compassion and justice if we do not first pay attention to where our compassion and justice is needed. It starts with our thoughts, which give rise to our words, which influence our deeds.

The reminder to pay attention to what you pay attention to also applies to how we pay attention to relationships and ourselves. When it comes to ourselves, it is important to pay attention to the marginalized parts of ourselves. By this I mean the vulnerable parts of ourselves that we prefer to hide from ourselves and from others—our sadness, anger, worry, stress, and shame. Ignoring these parts of ourselves comes at a high cost in terms of our health and wellness.

At any given time we each have areas of our life with which we are more or less satisfied. The chances are good that the areas where we satisfied are the areas that have been receiving our attention. The opposite of this is also true. If we are less satisfied with some area of our life, whether it be our work, a relationship, our health, our diet, our finances, or our spiritual life, it is most likely because we have not been focusing our attention on that area. We enjoy focusing our attention on the areas of our lives that are going well, and we tend to not want to focus attention on the areas with which we are less satisfied. It seems to be human nature to not want to pay attention to the areas of our lives that are not going well. A person who hasn't exercised in years will probably find it challenging to pay more attention to that area of his life. A couple who hasn't communicated well for a long time most likely will find it uncomfortable to start paying attention to that area of their life. A person who neglects keeping a budget and making good financial decisions will probably resist paying attention to that area of her life as well. We are all capable of minimizing and denying those areas of our lives that are not going well.

One potentially painful—and therefore often avoided—issue is unresolved grief. Unresolved grief, or what I often refer to as frozen grief, takes a large toll on a person's emotional and relational wellness, often without that person realizing it. Our modern culture seems to minimize grief and so, in turn, many people who have experienced loss do the same—they minimize their own grief. They try not to see or feel their feelings of sadness and vulnerability, which is another way of saying they try not to pay attention to it. The problem with not paying attention to grief is that healing cannot occur. Choosing to ignore or minimize grief will lead to disease in our body and dis-ease in our emotional wellness and relationships. When people pay attention to their grief it usually results in a short-term intensifying of their awareness of their sadness. Allowing themselves to feel and express this sadness, though, is what leads to healing in the long term. By paying attention to and honoring grief, it begins to heal.

The importance of what we pay attention to is crucial in relationships, too. When it comes to relationships it is important to pay attention to what it is you are noticing about your partner, friend, child, or colleague. Are you only noticing and amplifying the negative, hurtful things, the things that frustrate you about this person? Do you pay attention to the wonderful things about this person that make him special to you—things that may be all too easy to overlook and take for granted? Everyone is complicated and is a mixture of wonderful and less-than-wonderful characteristics. It's a matter of which aspects of their being we pay attention to that matters. *What* we pay attention to and *how* we pay attention to those we love will end up in large part determining the strength and health of those relationships.

Our spirituality influences our attention and our attention influences our well-being. Spirituality is primary here because it strongly shapes our attention. The connection between our spirituality and what and how we see the world is talked about in scripture and in some of the most well-known Christian hymns. "I once was blind, but now I see" from the hymn "Amazing Grace" does not refer to a recovery from literal blindness, but from the kind of blindness that comes from prejudice and the refusal to pay attention to the basic rights of human beings. The writer of that hymn began paying attention to a different aspect of the slave trade he was participating in and that made all the difference. It changed his life. You and I may not have conversions of perception as dramatic as that of the writer of "Amazing Grace," but we can choose to allow the Spirit to continuously expand and deepen what it is we pay attention to.

▶ Thought

As you read this reflection about paying attention, what thoughts does it raise for you?

What do you think about the idea that your spirituality has a strong influence on how and what you pay attention to?

▶ Word

This reflection talks about the importance of *how* we pay attention to other people. This often is revealed by our tone of voice, facial expressions, and body language. If you pause and pay attention to how you speak to people you care about, what do you notice?

Would you be willing to have a conversation with someone about a time when you had your "eyes opened" and you began to see an issue or a person in a different light?

Are you aware of any frozen or unresolved grief within yourself that you could pay more attention to by talking about it with someone else?

▶ Deed

Is there anyone in particular that you feel called to pay more attention to based on what you have experienced in reading this reflection?

Do you tend to pay more attention to positive or negative things around you? To strengthen your spiritual life, can you think of something you could do to focus more of your attention on the positive things you are grateful for?

Chapter 3

REST AND PLAY

Reflection 1

Assessing Rest and Play in Your Life

We now turn to Rest and Play, the second area of wellness related to the Soul in Living Compass. Whenever I lead a Living Compass small group program or a Living Compass retreat, this area of wellness seems to be discussed with the most feeling and frustration. What I hear in these discussions is that many people are learning through their self-assessment that this area of wellness in their lives is woefully out of balance.

I invite you to complete the Rest and Play self-assessment now, using the form provided in the appendix or online. When you are finished, transfer your number to the Rest and Play wedge of the compass tool on page 155.

All of Life is Interconnected

The good news is that because the Living Compass Self-Assessment Tool provides a snapshot of how you perceive your life today, change in your rest and play can be made starting today. One image I like to use to describe the results that come from the Living Compass self-assessments is to think of them as flowers in a garden. The areas of wellness that receive a lower score in the self-assessment are simply the areas of your garden that you have not been watering. These areas are a bit wilted from lack of attention. The areas where your scores are higher are, by contrast, the areas of your garden that you have been watering and tending to. Thus your wellness scores are merely indicators of what you have and have not been paying attention to.

Participants sometimes wonder why Rest and Play is included in the Soul part of the Living Compass and not in the Strength section, where physical wellness is addressed. The reason is that when I think of rest and play, I think of them in primarily spiritual terms. When I think of rest I am reminded of the practice within Judeo-Christian faiths of observing Sabbath. Three thousand years ago the biblical writers gave us the story of the Ten Commandments, and one of those commandments tells us to remember the Sabbath and to keep it holy. Another reflection in this retreat will deal more fully with this idea, but here it is important to note the significance of Sabbath time.

When someone asks if Rest and Play would fit better under Strength, it gives me an opportunity to explain how, in fact, all eight areas of wellness are interconnected. Each is connected to and affects the other. In fact, the way the Living Compass is drawn is misleading, because rather than having clear lines between the eight areas of wellness there really should be dotted lines, or better yet the eight areas should all be overlapping and intersecting.

To better understand the concept of how all the eight areas of wellness are connected and affect each other, let's reflect on how rest and play affects many of the other areas of wellness. Take the area of Handling Our Emotions, for example. If we neglect our need for rest and play for an extended period of time, it is quite likely that emotional wellness will be affected; emotions will be expressed by being irritable and cranky. If a person has been taking time to have enough rest and play in her life, she is likely to be more centered and calm, better equipped to express and handle her emotions in a positive manner.

Rest and play also have a strong effect on the Relationships area of the Living Compass. Play is one of the most essential ingredients in enhancing all kinds of relationships—friends, spouses, partners, parents and children, and families in general. Even within work relationships there is room for play as an essential team building activity. I believe that play is so important in relationships that one of the first questions I ask any couple or family that I am working with in counseling is how much and in what ways do they play and have fun together.

Rest and play also directly affect two additional areas of wellness in the Living Compass, namely Care for the Body and Stress Resiliency. We live in a culture where many people are sleep deprived. The health costs of inadequate sleep are clear and yet many people still cut corners where getting enough sleep is involved. And there is an obvious connection between sleep and stress. The more stress we have in our lives, the more trouble we will have sleeping. The more sleep we get, the more prepared we are to handle the demands of the day and the less stressed we will be, as getting more sleep will increase our ability to be resilient in the midst of stress. Increasing our stress resiliency, our ability to manage our stress, will help us to sleep better. Strengthening one area of wellness will positively affect the others, as they are all inter-connected.

I shared a story earlier about my three-year-old son trying to find my balance for me when I offhandedly told him, after I had fallen, that I had lost it. That story always reminds me that finding our balance is ultimately our responsibility. It is just as misguided for us to expect others to find it for us as it was for my son to think that he could find my balance in the bushes that day. We do know that rest and play are essential factors to finding and creating balance in our lives and can be helpful tools to finding it for ourselves.

What I often hear from Living Compass participants is that their lives are out of balance and that being out of balance is directly related to and evidenced by their low scores in Rest and Play. No one else can find the time for rest and play for us. Rest and play can only be created as we make the commitment to be intentional about including these two essential components in our balanced life. The tricky part is that all of life is interconnected; you may need to evaluate your priorities and change other things in your life to make room for this important part of your wellness. Examining priorities and keeping them in focus is an important part of creating wellness.

▶ Thought

What thoughts or feelings did the Rest and Play self-assessment bring up for you?

This reflection talks about how rest and play are connected and affect many other areas of a person's wellness. How is this true in your own life or for others you know? What other areas of the Compass do you think are affected by rest and play, either positively or negatively?

▶ Word

Is there a relationship in your life that could benefit from a little more play time? If so, would you be willing to have a conversation with that person discussing your interest in playing more with them and what you could do together?

Would you be willing to ask others if they see you as a fun-loving person or a person who knows how to rest? How do you imagine others in your life would answer this question?

▶ Deed

The self-assessment asks if you feel that you are overly connected to email, TV, Internet, smartphone, computer, and other technologies. Based on how you scaled yourself on this, would you like to make any changes going forward?

Do you have a hobby? Would you like to spend more time doing this hobby? Is there a new hobby you might like to try?

Are there changes you want to make to get enough rest and sleep?

Reflection 2

Rest for Our Souls

The Bible has quite a few passages that speak of the importance of rest. One of Jesus' clearest statements about rest is found in the eleventh chapter of Matthew.

> Come to me, all you that are weary and are carrying heavy burdens, and I will give you rest. Take my yoke upon you, and learn from me; for I am gentle and humble in heart, and you will find rest for your souls. For my yoke is easy, and my burden is light. (Matthew 11:28–30)

I believe one of the reasons these words speak to us so powerfully today is that Jesus understands who we are. He gets us. He knows that we are often weary and are often carrying burdens. We hear these words and feel that Jesus is speaking directly to us. How does he know that this is exactly how I am feeling right now?

So, knowing that we are burdened, what does he have to offer us? The answer is simple. He offers us rest. Not just any kind of rest: he is specific in saying that the rest he offers us is rest for our souls.

Rest for the soul sounds like something we probably want, but what exactly is it? We know what rest for our bodies feels like, but what does rest for our souls feel like? For me, the word that comes closest to describing rest for the soul is the word "serenity." Serenity for me means that I am at peace with my life as it is, living in the present moment and appreciating it for what it is. To live with serenity is to live with acceptance of what is. It is to let go of control and worry. Not that this is something I experience often or easily, but it is an ideal for which I strive.

Twelve-step groups such as Alcoholics Anonymous talk about serenity a great deal. In fact, the Serenity Prayer, while not written specifically for Alcoholics Anonymous, has become the signature prayer of that organization. The opening of the Serenity Prayer is well known, even to people who have never been connected with a twelve-step group.

> God, grant me the serenity to accept the things I cannot change;
> the courage to change the things I can;
> and wisdom to know the difference.

This prayer is in alignment with the words of Jesus quoted earlier. Both Jesus' words and this prayer make it clear that rest and serenity are gifts that come from God. Rest for the soul is not something we *make* happen as much as it is something that we *let* happen. It is a gift that is freely offered to us, but like any gift, we must take the time to open the gift and receive it.

Rest in Peace

The phrase "may they rest in peace" is widely spoken when someone has just died. It is so common that we even recognize it just by its initials, "R.I.P." Rest in peace is offered as a prayer and a hope for the soul of the person who has just passed away.

But what if we were to pray this prayer for those we love, as well as for ourselves, when we are all still very much alive? Wouldn't it be wonderful if "rest in peace" was something that we sought in the here-and-now, not just in the hereafter? Resting in peace is what our souls truly desire and what I believe God wants for us now.

While this resting in peace, this rest for the soul, is a gift offered from God, there are practices and habits that will help maximize our ability to receive this gift. In an earlier reflection in the Spirituality section of this retreat, I wrote about a centering prayer practice called "Receive and Release." In that reflection I described this kind of centering prayer as "resting in God." A regular habit of praying this centering prayer, or any other kind of prayer or meditation that quiets the mind, will help us experience this rest for our souls.

One of the benefits of giving our bodies the rest they need is that it will, in turn, make our bodies stronger. Adequate rest for our bodies means that when we need our bodies to be strong, they will be ready to perform at their best. The same is true when it comes to seeking rest for our souls. Adequate rest for your soul means that when you are going through a hard time or are faced with a challenge and need for your soul to be strong, it will be ready.

I think of our souls being ready to act as related to the second part of the Serenity Prayer, having "courage to change the things I can." Our souls need to be strong to take on the things that need to be changed in our own lives and in the world. And just as with our bodies, in order for our souls to be strong we need to be sure that they also have adequate rest.

I mentioned centering prayer as one way to find rest and peace for our souls, but there are as many unique ways to find this rest and peace as there are unique souls. For many people worship creates rest for their soul. Others find that music, time in nature, time in solitude, time with loved ones, time to create, and simply time to sleep help to create rest for their souls. What is most important is not how we seek this rest and peace for our souls, but that we are sure to make time to do so.

For everything there is a season and a time for every matter. There is a time to be active and a time to rest. There is a time to do and a time to be. There is a time to act with courage to change that which needs to be changed, and there is a time to receive the gift of serenity so that we can accept the things we cannot change.

▶ Thought

What does "rest for the soul" mean to you? Do you know this feeling in your own life?

How does the term "serenity" or the opening lines of the Serenity Prayer speak to you about rest for your soul?

▶ Word

This reflection shares some words from the Bible and some words from the well-known Serenity Prayer that touch on rest for the soul. What words might you use to describe rest for the soul? Are there other words from the Bible or quotations or prayers that you find helpful in describing this kind of rest?

The opening scripture in this reflection speaks of "feeling weary" and "carrying heavy burdens." Do these phrases describe you in any way right now? If so, is there someone you would be willing to share a word or a conversation with about what you are experiencing?

▶ Deed

Many different habits or practices are mentioned as commonly helping people to experience rest for their souls. What practices, habits, or activities help you experience rest for your soul?

Are you interested in trying a new practice or habit to help create "rest in peace" in the here-and-now? Is there something you need to let go of to allow you to better "rest in peace"? What changes do you think would benefit your wellness in this area?

Reflection 3

We Don't Stop Playing Because We Grow Old, We Grow Old Because We Stop Playing

The title of this reflection is a quotation from the Irish playwright George Bernard Shaw. We shared this quotation on our Living Compass Facebook page along with a photo of a couple on the beach with their long pants rolled up to their knees, dancing in the surf. This post received far more "likes" and "shares" than any of the several hundred other similar quotations and photos we had previously posted.

So the question this begs, of course, is why did this one post get so much interest? I think the reason is that most people have more than enough seriousness in their lives and what many of us desire and need is more fun and playfulness. A few people responded to the photo with comments such as, "I wish had the time or money to go on a beach vacation like that, but that's not going to happen anytime soon." For these people, the photo might have, unfortunately, created more stress and seriousness than playfulness!

Perhaps it would be helpful if we expanded our understanding of playfulness to include much more than merely going on a vacation. I believe that playfulness is not primarily something we do, but is rather an attitude, an outlook on life that we choose. Being playful is a choice. In many situations and endeavors, we can choose to bring either a serious or a playful energy and outlook to the situation. I know for myself, the attitude I bring to any conversation has a direct impact on all those around me. If I am grumpy and serious, the conversation will most likely be tense and constricted. If I decide instead to start the conversation with humor and good will, the conversation will be lighter and more expansive and those of us participating in the conversation are likely to feel that way, as well.

Mother Teresa once wrote that people should not worry about whether they are doing many great, heroic acts of love in their lives, but rather they should focus on doing the little things with great love. This seems to work regarding the importance of play, as well. Let's not wait for some big, special vacation to play—or even for the day off or the weekend. Let's find a way to bring playfulness into all of the little things we do each day.

Of course, some things we do and some situations we encounter are very serious. Most of time though, there is room for us to bring a greater spirit of playfulness into our lives and into our relationships. Think for a moment about people who energize you by their presence. I would guess that they are people who have a good balance of playfulness and seriousness in their lives and in their interactions with you and others.

The good feeling we get from the photo of the couple playing in the waves reminds us how important it is to take time to be playful. Frolicking in the breaking ocean waves comes pretty easily for most of us. We will most likely have to work a little harder to keep a playful attitude in the midst of the waves of stress that break fairly regularly in our daily lives. Life is indeed quite serious at times, but it also presents more opportunities to be playful than we may notice.

Playing Well with Others
One of the gifts of having cultivated a playful spirit is that it often leads us to playful activities with others. Just as laughing and letting your hair down is good for the soul, it is good for relationships, too. Play opens our hearts and souls and creates the opportunity for deeper connections. In romantic relationships, one obvious and powerful expression of play involves sexu-

ality. Sexual intimacy is a form of play, connecting hearts, souls, and bodies in a deeply soulful manner.

Play and laughter is probably most often associated with children. After all, it is children who have "play dates" and it is children who ask, "Can I play with Sarah today?" Indeed, children can bring out the playful spirit in most adults, helping us to let loose. There is great joy in watching an adult giggling with a baby. It's hard to know who is enjoying the interaction more—the baby or the adult.

When I served as a full-time pastor, one of the most popular activities we had at church was not an overtly religious one. The most popular activity was the semiannual all-church game night. Our game nights included people of all ages, from toddlers to people in their nineties. Every person who came was encouraged to bring a game they loved to play and then invite others in attendance to play it with them. This created wonderful intergenerational evenings for all, with folks of all ages gathered around playing games and having fun together. *Candyland, Risk, Cranium, Scrabble, Clue,* and Bridge were all being played at different tables. People would rotate and learn new games and meet new friends in the process. While game nights were not religious in nature, they were good for the souls of those who participated!

Children have something else important to teach us about play. They teach us that play need not be complicated or expensive. We adults sometimes think we need expensive toys or expensive trips to provide fun. Children, on the other hand, remind us that something as simple as playing with a cardboard box can create hours of fun.

I was reminded of the joy of simple and spontaneous play recently when my nephew told me he had just spent an entire afternoon with his two-and-a-half-year-old son making a pirate ship out of a couple of cardboard boxes. The cost for this amazing experience? Nothing. The benefits from this experience? Priceless. My nephew and his son did more than just create a pirate ship on a Saturday afternoon. They also strengthened their already amazing relationship, rekindled their imaginations, and created wonderful memories. Talk about creating wellness!

Play is good for the soul no matter our age as it renews our spirits and strengthens our relationships. Three thousand years ago, people knew that play and the cheerfulness it creates was good for one's health, for it was at that time that the writer of the book of Proverbs wrote, "A cheerful heart is a good medicine" (Proverbs 17:22).

▶ Thought

Do you think of yourself as a person who "plays well with others"?

What does the saying "We don't stop playing because we grow old, we grow old because we stop playing" mean to you?

▶ **Word**

What words and messages did the adults in your life give to you about play when you were growing up? Was it valued as important? Did you see the adults in your life have a healthy way to play?

What words come to mind when you think of playing? Wasting time? Goofing off? Making time for something important? An important part of enjoying the world God has created? Others?

▶ **Deed**

Would you like more time to play in your life? If so, what could you do to make this happen?

When it comes to playing, is there something new you would like to try, such as a new hobby or a new way of recreating? What would you need to do to make this happen?

Do you play in ways that are good for your overall wellness? What might you do to play differently so that it enhances the rest of your life as well?

Reflection 4

Sharpening Our Saws

In 1989 Stephen Covey wrote a book entitled *The Seven Habits of Highly Effective People*. The book has sold over 25 million copies and is one of the most popular self-help books of all time. The seventh habit that Covey speaks of is the habit of "sharpening our saws." It is based on a well-known story, and I believe it is an essential aspect of rest and play.

The story that reminds us of the importance of sharpening our saws is about two lumberjacks. These two lumberjacks are near the end of a long day, cutting down large trees since just after sun-up, using an old fashioned two-person hand saw, with one of them on each end pulling back and forth. As the day comes to a close, a passerby happens upon the two lumberjacks and pauses to watch them work their craft. The passerby looks around and sees dozens of large trees that have been felled just that day, but at the same time notices that the lumberjacks are making absolutely no progress on the last tree of the day. They are half-way through the tree and no matter how hard they work, they cannot cut through this last tree. The two men finally call it quits and strike up a conversation with the passerby. They point proudly to all the trees that they had cut that day, explaining that the last few trees have taken them twice as long to cut, and that the last tree was impossible for them to topple. They were frustrated and perplexed as to why this was, and assumed it was because they were worn out from all the effort they had exerted. It was just then that the passerby asked them the key question: "I'm just curious, did you ever take time during the day to stop and sharpen your saw?"

The two lumberjacks were so busy working that they had forgotten to take time to sharpen the saw. They were probably working just as hard in the afternoon as they had been in the morning, perhaps even harder, but were less and less effective as the day wore on. And not only were they less effective, but they ended the day feeling discouraged. Their last experience of the day was one of failure because they were not able to get through that final tree.

In my work as a spiritual director and retreat leader, I find that many people come for spiritual direction or on a retreat because they feel like these two lumberjacks felt at the end of the day. People seeking out an opportunity for spiritual direction or a retreat are often on the edge of burn out. They are exhausted spiritually, physically, and emotionally. They have been "sawing" with more and more effort, but are frustrated with how ineffective they are being and feeling. The "sawing" may be different for each person—a parent of young children who is overwhelmed by trying to do it all, a teacher who brings three hours of work home every night, a person working several jobs to make ends meet, a student juggling school and work, a business owner who works twelve-hour days trying to make payroll, an overworked medical professional, a clergy person working seven days a week, or a caretaker who never gets a break from caring for a loved one—they are all alike in that they are on the edge of burning out.

The first thing people who are exhausted are seeking is of course rest—rest for their bodies, rest for their souls, and rest for their minds. They soon discover, though, that they are seeking more than just rest, they are seeking something to give them new energy, something to help them re-create themselves. They discover that, in addition to rest, they also need to "sharpen their saw." It is important to note that there is a distinction here, as these are two different needs.

In the story of the two lumberjacks, clearly they neglected both their need for rest and their need to sharpen the saw. Doing both would have made them more productive and allowed them to end the day feeling good about their efforts. If the lumberjacks had simply taken time to rest, although it would have been helpful, it would not have been enough. These lumberjacks also needed to take time to sharpen their saw. It's an important lesson for all of us.

Making time for "down time" and rest is important, but it is not the same as recreation that sharpens the saw. I enjoy resting on the couch and watching a TV show or ballgame as much as the next person, but over time I have realized that this does little to "sharpen my saw," nor is it recreational for me. When I truly want to sharpen my saw I know that I need do something intentional and active. I might go for a walk, run, or bike ride, read an inspiring book, get together with some close friends for some great conversation, or work in the garden, cook a nice meal, engage in a favorite hobby, or spend time in prayer or meditation. It is my experience that many people fail to see the important difference between merely resting and doing things that are re-creational, things that actively renew their physical, spiritual, and emotional energy.

Forms of true recreation are activities that sharpen our saws. It is interesting to note that the word "recreation" literally means "re-creation." To create is to be intentional and active in what we are doing to produce something new. Thus, in order to re-create in ways that sharpen our saws we need to be intentional and active so that we will be renewed. Simply watching television, for example, may be restful in the short term but may not be re-creative.

What Makes Our Saws Become Dull

While it is important to note what truly sharpens our saws, it is also helpful to reflect on what contributes to our saws losing their sharp edge. In this context, I am especially aware of one thing in particular that is touted as being recreational and which, I believe, can ultimately do just the opposite, and that is alcohol. I see many people using alcohol and other drugs in their lives, espousing it as their tool to relax and unwind; it is their way to recreate. We are bombarded with media messages that connect having a good time with consuming alcohol, messages that seem to connect consuming alcohol with recreation. We need to be mindful of our use of alcohol and other drugs, as they can easily end up having a negative impact on our all-around wellness. If we are not careful, they can dull our saws over time.

Research shows that alcohol is fine in moderation, when used as a beverage, for most people. Through years of my professional observations, though, I believe that regularly consuming alcohol in larger amounts works to make our saws dull and actually lowers physical, spiritual, and emotional energy.

People can easily think of the "high" of using alcohol or drugs as being re-creative, especially if they are tired and stressed. If they wake up more exhausted the next day than they were the night before, a vicious cycle can begin. Because the person is now more exhausted, he seeks out another little "pick me up" to re-energize himself. This, of course, does not last long either and soon an addictive cycle is created; feeling tired and stressed, seeking relief through alcohol, feeling tired and stress, seeking relief, and so on. Food can, of course, be used in the same way as alcohol and drugs, as a way to try and fill emotional and spiritual needs

So when it comes to remembering the importance of sharpening our saws, we need to keep two things in mind. First, we need to remember to do it! Second, we need to be sure that our re-creational activities are truly sharpening our saws.

▶ Thought

What are your thoughts related to the story about the two lumberjacks and the need to "sharpen our saws"? Can you make any connections to your life?

Does this reflection cause you to think differently about how you recreate?

▶ Word

Talk about something you have done recently that was truly re-creative for you. What made this such a good experience for you?

Our recreational activities often involve our friends and/or family. If we want to begin a new way of recreating, or change a way we have been recreating, we may need to have a conversation with a friend or family member to involve them in this change. Can you think of a conversation like this that you might want to have with a friend or family member?

▶ Deed

In light of this reflection, is there anything different you want to do to help sharpen your saw?

Is there anything you want to stop doing or to do differently, something you now realize does not help you in sharpening your saw?

Reflection 5

Laughing Well

I love to laugh, so it is probably not a coincidence that the people I love spending time with are the people with whom I laugh the most. Stop and think for a moment in your own life about experiences you have had with others where you laughed out loud with abandon, experiences which made you double over in laughter. Chances are you remember and tell the stories of those experiences for years, as they are so much fun!

The frequency of laughter in our lives, as well as the frequency of those kinds of humorous experiences that we remember for a long time, is a good measure of the amount of rest and play we are enjoying in our lives. The opposite of this is true as well. When I notice that I am not laughing much that is a whisper to me that I may be in need of some fun, some rest and play to help alleviate my seriousness and get me back in balance.

I believe that the number one warning sign that we need more rest and play in our lives is when we start taking ourselves, our interactions with others, and our work too seriously. Now, I am the first to acknowledge that there is a time to be serious in life. Life puts us in very serious situations on occasion. There is a difference, however, between being serious and taking ourselves too seriously. Much of life is serious and needs our concentrated attention and respect. By using the phrase "taking ourselves too seriously" I am instead referring to the tendency of many of us to be serious when we simply do not need to be. At these times, we need to lighten up.

In my experience most people do not need to be reminded to take themselves and their lives more seriously. My experience is quite the opposite. I see most people needing help to take themselves and their concerns a bit less seriously, letting go of their concerns and focusing their attention instead on gaining a helpful perspective, strengthening their faith that all will be taken care of in time.

Edwin Friedman, a rabbi, family therapist, and leadership expert who died in 1996, wrote a great deal about anxiety and stress within relationships. He believed that seriousness within any person, relationship, or organization was a warning sign of underlying anxiety and stress. He believed that the likelihood of people becoming too serious rose in direct proportion to the amount of unresolved anxiety and stress they were experiencing in their lives and in their relationships.

From years of conversations in my professional life with all kinds of people, I think Friedman's insight into the connection between seriousness and anxiety is right on target. I have seen this to be true in families as well as in congregations. I have also observed things within myself that confirm this belief for me. When I am living with unresolved stress or anxiety for any prolonged length of time, I inevitably become very serious and find very little to be funny. And because I completely lose my sense of humor when I get this serious, any attempt by someone to use humor to try and get me to relax a little bit will not go well. Their attempt to reach out to me is almost always met with some kind of defensive remark on my part. "Don't you realize how serious and important this is? I can't afford to relax for one moment until this is resolved!"

Have you ever known a person or a relationship that appears always to be serious, where there is little room for laughter? It is as if the individual involved has the weight of the world on his shoulders and can't possibly lighten up until "x" or "y" gets resolved. If you know someone with this tendency, you may have already noticed that over time there is always a new "x" or "y" that pops up as a new barrier to his being able to lighten up. This person seems to chronically be unable to allow himself to be less serious about his circumstances and to enjoy the pleasures of life.

I have seen this tendency in organizations as well, where the culture of a business or a congregation seems to bless being quite serious, especially in its leaders. In an organization with this ethos a leader may not be considered a real leader unless she is feeling overwhelmed and tired—in other words, unless she is serious most of the time. At its worst this kind of seriousness seems to be worn as a badge of honor, serving as a validation of how hard the leader is working. You can detect this tendency easily in an organization by the lack of laughter and fun.

Here again, I believe that Edwin Friedman is right on target. I believe that a leader who is chronically serious is a leader who is on the way to burning out and one who is not facing and resolving the stress that exists either within himself or the system he is leading. Not only is he on the way to burning out, so is the system. In this situation, the first thing the leader needs to learn to do is manage his own anxiety. If he does this, he will be better able to address and manage the anxiety within the system he is leading. As long as he is mirroring the same kind of seriousness and anxiety that is in the system, he will not be able to facilitate the necessary change within the system. I have found that all of what I have just said is true not just of leaders in the workplace, but of leaders in all relational systems, including families.

Please remember that the seriousness I am talking about here is what we have in mind when we say to someone (or to ourselves), "Stop taking yourself so seriously." We would not say this to someone who just received a devastating diagnosis. We would say it to a person is always striving for perfection and is wearing herself and others out in the process.

As I mentioned briefly before, I have a tendency to take myself too seriously sometimes. I describe myself as a "recovering perfectionist," although that recovery is still a work in progress. My adult children have a word they say to me whenever they experience me taking things a little too seriously. They simply touch my arm and say, "Breathe." Because this has happened so many times, this very word cracks us all up and we begin to laugh and soon my seriousness is cured.

Rest, play, and humor are great cures for seriousness. The next time you are thinking that you need to take yourself less seriously you can try one or any combination of these three. Laughter and tension cannot exist in the body at the same time. Laughter and seriousness cannot exist within our hearts and souls at the same time. And laughter, it turns out, is good for the brain too, as it releases endorphins and creates greater oxygen flow to the brain. Maybe my children know more than I ever realized when they tell me to "breathe" whenever I take myself too seriously.

I quoted above the great verse from the book of Proverbs that speaks of how good laughter is for our souls: "A cheerful heart is a good medicine, but a downcast spirit dries up the bones" (Proverbs 17:22). Cheerful hearts are contagious. We are attracted to and want to be around people with cheerful dispositions. On the other hand, a "downcast spirit" is also contagious and over time we will likely distance ourselves from people or organizations that are stuck in their downcast spirit.

Have you ever heard of the tradition of a church celebrating Holy Humor Sunday? In some churches it's known as Laughter Sunday or Bright Sunday. It is typically celebrated the Sunday after Easter. If you search the Internet for "Holy Humor Sunday" you will find a host of prayers, jokes, and readings for use on that Sunday. This tradition is a great reminder that laughter is good for the soul.

▶ Thought

Do you think of yourself as having a good sense of humor? Do you think of yourself as someone who laughs a lot?

What do you think of the idea that being overly serious is a symptom of unresolved anxiety or stress?

▶ Word

Just as an individual can at times lose her sense of humor, so can a relationship. Is there a relationship in your life where you would like to see more humor and lightness?

Will you have a conversation with that person to begin to create the change you are seeking?

▶ Deed

Is there an organization or congregation of which you are a part where you would like to experience more laughter? What can you do to help make this happen?

When do you tend to laugh the most, and what might you do differently to increase these experiences of laughter?

Living Well With All Your
MIND

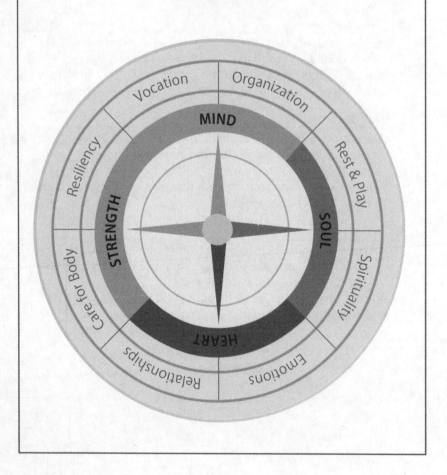

Chapter 4

VOCATION

Reflection 1

Assessing Your Vocational Wellness

In our Living Compass Wellness program we use the word "vocation" in a very broad sense. This is initially confusing for some people because it can be defined to have a more narrow meaning. The narrow understanding associates vocation with a pastor, priest, or nun who is called to religious life and service.

We encourage you instead to consider a broader definition of vocation as you work through this retreat. At Living Compass, we believe that everyone has a vocation, as a vocation has to do with the way each of us understands our life's purpose. Whether we are conscious of it or not, whether we can clearly articulate it or not, most of us have an overall sense of purpose in our life. With this in mind, the reflections offered in this section of the retreat dealing with vocation are designed to help clarify and articulate your sense of purpose for your life.

I invite you to complete the Vocation self-assessment now, using the form provided in the appendix or online. When you are finished, transfer your number to the Vocation wedge of the compass tool on page 155. Remember there are no "right" or "wrong" answers, or "good" or "bad" scores. The scores simply reveal a sense of how you see your vocational wellness at this moment.

Your Personal Mission Statement

Most businesses, nonprofit organizations, and churches have a mission statement. These mission statements are usually created by a core group of leaders or the organization's founders. Though they may be tweaked from time to time, these statements usually remain fairly consistent over the lifetime of an organization. Mission statements succinctly state the unique purpose of the organization. They answer the "Why?" question of the organization's existence and what it hopes to accomplish. These statements both arise from and continue to shape the unique identity of the organization. You could say that a mission statement serves as an orienting compass for an organization.

The mission statement of the YMCA, for example, is, "To put Christian principles into practice through programs that build a healthy spirit, mind and body for all." While the mission of the YMCA endures over time, the specific programs it offers to fulfill its mission are changing to suit the needs of the people it is serving and in response to an ever-changing world.

Starbucks Coffee Company has a mission statement. "Our mission: to inspire and nurture the human spirit—one person, one cup and one neighborhood at a time." Here we see a very broad mission statement that speaks to an interest in the human spirit, while only tangentially referring to its primary product, coffee. You could think of a mission statement as reflecting an organization's vocation. The mission statement defines and directs its purpose, its reason for being in the world.

What if you were to write a mission statement for your life? What might it say? What would it include? It is safe to say that if you created a mission statement for your life it would be a good description of how you understand your vocation, your life purpose.

A personal mission statement would express how you intend to live your deepest beliefs in the world. A personal mission statement would speak to the intersection between your unique gifts and the needs of the world in which you live. It would need to be broad enough to endure over time. And as we saw with the mission statements from the YMCA and Starbucks Coffee Company, personal mission statements, yours included, need to leave room for flexibility, so that over time new ways are embraced in an attempt to continue to live out the mission. Different times and stages of your life will require new ways of doing things, but your life mission may not.

A personal mission statement might look like this. "My mission in life is to continue to develop the gifts that God has given me so that I can be an instrument for creating peace, love, and abundance in the world, beginning with myself, extending to my important relationships, and then to the wider world." This mission statement includes at least three important principles.

First: It says the person will continue to develop the unique gifts that he has been given.

Second: It defines the purpose for developing these gifts, namely to create peace, love, and abundance in the world.

Third: This statement defines who this person hopes to affect directly from these gifts of peace, love, and abundance toward—self, loved ones, and the larger community.

Personal mission statements guide individuals in both their personal and in their work life. Vocation is not merely something we do in our work or public life. Instead it is integrated into all aspects of life—personal, family, work, and community. The Living Compass wellness philosophy is holistic in nature, based on the integral understanding that all areas of wellness are interconnected. We can see that concept of interconnectedness when we observe the relationship between spirituality and vocation. It has been my observation over the years that when people are invited to write their own personal mission statements, they almost always ground their mission statements in their faith. Vocation is the outward and visible expression of a person's spirituality and understanding of one's place in God's world.

Our sense of vocation, then, along with our faith, serves as a compass to orient both big and small decisions. Having a clear sense of mission and vocation provides an important filter through which to run important decisions. *Does this action, this choice, or this decision align with my mission, my vocation in life?* This is a question well worth keeping in the forefront of our minds.

As you read and interact with the remaining four reflections on vocation, I hope you will work to define your unique purpose and mission in life with a renewed clarity. Keep in mind that with your unique gifts, along with your unique experience, you can uniquely affect the world. You can make a difference!

When an organization holds a retreat for its leaders, it is common to take time to look again at the organization's mission statement and to reflect on how closely aligned the organization's activities are with that mission statement. This retreat offers you the opportunity to do the same thing for yourself.

▶ Thought

What thoughts and feelings did the Vocation self-assessment bring up for you? You might want to write some of them down in your journal.

This reflection talks about a strong connection between spirituality and vocation. Do you see this connection in your own life?

▶ Word

What words come to mind when describing your sense of your vocation in the world?

Is there someone you would be willing to talk with about new ways you can use your unique gifts and experience to help strengthen your sense of vocation?

▶ Deed

As you reflect on the many activities in your life, are there a few
specific activities that truly express your sense of your vocation
and mission? If so, what are those things and what can you
learn from them as you clarify your understanding of your
vocation?

This reflection talks about creating a personal mission statement.
If you have not already done so, would you be willing to
experiment with writing a personal mission statement? Would
you be willing to share it with others?

Reflection 2

Just Bring Yourself

Recently some dear friends invited my wife and me to a dinner party. The
invitation came via email and explained that it would be a casual night of
cooking and catching up. When I inquired about what we could bring the
answer was, "Just bring yourself." Having vocational wellness on my mind
that day, I thought to myself that their answer was unintentionally great
advice for all of us. To know and to be able to bring our true selves to
everything we do is the foundation of vocational wellness. Just bring yourself.

There is a great three-hundred-year-old story that makes this same
point. Rabbi Zusya was a wise Hasidic master who lived in Poland in the
eighteenth century. A story is told that a student once asked him, "Rabbi
Zusya, what if when you die and go to heaven, God asks you why were
you not more like Moses?" Wise Zusya thought for a moment, and answered, "The question God might have for me is not why was I not more
like Moses, but why was I not more like Zusya."

This story gets at the heart of the meaning of vocational wellness. Vocational wellness has to do with how we are expressing and using our true
selves in the world. Aspects of our unique selves are in evidence whenever
we interact with the world: the way we contribute to our families and
friendships, the work we do, the volunteer work we offer to our community, church, school, or nonprofit, and our various hobbies and interests.
Each of these offers us a chance to express our true selves and gives voice
to what matters most to us.

Actually, the word "vocation" comes from the same root word as
"vocal," or "voice." A vocation then can be thought of in two ways related
to this meaning: first, we must listen to God's voice, and second, we must

develop our sense of voice in the world. Our true vocation in life is the response we make to the voice of the God who has created us. What is the voice of the One who created us calling us to be or to become? How can we use our unique gifts in God's service? To answer these questions requires that we spend time listening to that voice and then discerning how we might act on what we hear.

Here, again, we see the connection between vocation and spirituality. One of the purposes of engaging in spiritual practices, for example, is to be still so that we can hear God's voice. We need to be still in order to hear God's call, God's desired direction for us. Because an essential aspect of vocation is responding to God's voice in our lives, we must make time and space to listen to that voice on an ongoing basis. There are many voices in our lives calling for our attention; it is important to learn what voices to pay attention to and which to ignore. It takes intentional effort and practice to pay attention to and discern the voice of God in the midst of all the noise around us.

The notion of "paying attention to what you pay attention to" is quite applicable here. The earlier reflection "What Makes Your Face Shine?" in the section on Spirituality also clearly related to vocation. When you listen to people talk about their work, their volunteer work, their roles with family and friends, or their hobbies, watch for what makes their face shine. It is most likely an important clue to how they understand their vocation in the world.

There is a second way in which the root meaning of vocation as voice can be helpful to our understanding and living into our vocation: To develop one's sense of vocation also is to develop one's sense of voice in the world. It is not uncommon to hear someone say, for example, "I feel like I'm finding my own voice or my own style as a _____." It could be finding one's voice as a parent, an artist, in a career, as a leader, or a volunteer. Discovering, clarifying, and strengthening one's voice is an essential part of living out one's sense of vocation.

Whenever we take on a new role in life, it is natural for us to imitate others who have filled that role before us. When I first became a pastor, my preaching style imitated some of the pastors who had been my mentors and teachers. When I first became a father, I imitated fathers I admired and tried to be like them. But as we grow more comfortable with a new role, we begin to find and develop our own voices. To develop one's unique voice in the world is vitally important in developing a sense of peace where vocational wellness is involved.

All of this comes together in a phrase from pastor and author Frederick Buechner. He writes that your vocation, your purpose in life, "is where your deep gladness and the world's deep hunger meet."* While this ideal

---

* Frederick Buechner, *Wishful Thinking: A Theological ABC* (New York: HarperCollins, 1993), 93.

may never fully or finally be attained, it is a wonderful way to describe what we are striving for when it comes to vocational wellness.

Your vocation may or may not overlap with your job. Your vocation may be more fully expressed through volunteer service, or through your relationships with your family, friends, neighbors or faith community. Once we have a clear sense of our vocation, we need to find ways to express it no matter where we find ourselves. When we are living out of our unique God-given gifts and passions, we feel alive, excited, and thoroughly engaged with the world. It is our responsibility to find outlets for these gifts to fill a need in the world, for the common good.

There is a beautiful biblical reading that speaks directly to vocation. This passage speaks to the varieties of gifts that have been given by the Spirit to all of us. Each of these unique gifts is related to our unique voice in the world. As you read this passage, take a moment to reflect on some of the unique gifts that the Spirit has given you alone.

> Now there are varieties of gifts, but the same Spirit; and there are varieties of services, but the same Lord; and there are varieties of activities, but it is the same God who activates all of them in everyone. To each is given the manifestation of the Spirit for the common good. To one is given through the Spirit the utterance of wisdom, and to another the utterance of knowledge according to the same Spirit, to another faith by the same Spirit, to another gifts of healing by the one Spirit, to another the working of miracles, to another prophecy, to another the discernment of spirits, to another various kinds of tongues, to another the interpretation of tongues. All these are activated by one and the same Spirit, who allots to each one individually just as the Spirit chooses. (1 Corinthians 12:4–11)

The title of this section, "Just Bring Yourself," sounds so simple, and yet just being ourselves is often more difficult than we may at first realize. We often advise someone anxious about a meeting or going on a job interview, "Just be yourself, and you will be fine." When we give this advice we probably mean that they are wonderful as they are and if they just let that show, the other will love them as we do. But being ourselves is both the simplest and the hardest thing, for that person heading into a job interview and for us in our day-to-day lives. It is often the work of a lifetime to fully learn what it means to be truly, authentically ourselves, but it is well worth the effort as our faces shine and the world becomes a little brighter place.

▶ Thought

How do you think about vocation and vocational wellness? Does thinking about vocation as being related to the words "voice" and "vocal" make sense to you and help clarify your understanding of vocation?

Do you think you can live out a vocation even if you don't really enjoy your job? How could that be?

▶ Word

We often discover and clarify the Spirit's call to us in community with others. Who might you talk with about how you are hearing the Spirit's voice in your life right now?

If you were to articulate your sense of vocation in your life right now, what words might you say?

▶ Deed

This reflection makes a connection between our sense of vocation and what makes our faces shine. At this point in your life, what activities and/or what roles in your life make your face shine?

Is there something new you might like to do, something new you might like to try, that might help you more fully express your sense of vocation in your life? If so, what it that? Might you share this idea with others? What first step might you take to try to do this?

Reflection 3

The Scripts and Stories of Our Lives

We Americans love to go to the movies. Over the last ten years alone, Americans have purchased an average of 1.4 billion movie tickets each year, resulting in average annual movie ticket revenue of $10.5 billion. These numbers do not reflect the additional sales and viewing numbers of other movie sources such as DVDs and online viewing. Movies are clearly an important part of our culture!

In many ways, movies have become a primary way our culture tells the stories of our time. Like stories, movies come in every genre imaginable. Some movies are simply for entertainment, while others embody and teach important values about character, relationships, and meaning.

It takes the creative work of many talented people to produce a movie. In fact, the Oscar statue, the coveted award given to winners at the

Academy Awards every year, has a five sprocket movie reel on its base to symbolize the five professions that work together to create a movie: actors, writers, directors, producers, and technicians. While each of these is essential in the making of a movie, the whole process starts with the writer. Without a writer, without a script, none of the other roles would ever be needed.

Have you ever stopped to wonder if someone made a movie of your life, what it would be like? What would it be called? Would it be a comedy, drama, tragedy, or mystery? Now imagine that because this is the story of your life, only you can be the scriptwriter for this film. What would you write? What details would you be sure to include? What details would you want to leave out? Would you play yourself or would you cast someone else in the lead role?

It is fairly safe to say that none of us will actually ever be asked to write a script about our life for Hollywood, but the truth is, you and I are writing the scripts of our lives each and every day. Day by day we make the same kinds of decisions about our lives that scriptwriters make about their movies. Who will be the main characters in our scripts? Will the relationships between the lead actor and the other cast members be marked by compassion or conflict? How will the lead actor and his or her significant relationships evolve over time, and what kind of character development will there be? What values and belief systems will influence the choices that the lead actor and the other characters make?

When we are young, other people are the primary scriptwriters for our lives, influencing our lives in innumerable ways. Our families, along with our culture, write important details into our scripts and subsequent belief systems: our identity, where we grow up, what it means to be a boy or girl, what loving relationships look like, whether others can be trusted or not, and what gives life its greatest meaning and purpose. Our spirituality is deeply formed and influenced by the early "scriptwriters" in our lives as well.

A turning point begins to emerge in adolescence and young adulthood, which helps to explain why this is often a tumultuous time in families. Young people begin the awkward transition to adulthood by first beginning to make their own choices about the scripts and stories of their lives. They begin to experiment with not just being a character in someone else's script, but trying out a leading role in their own story. They begin to decide what "characters" they will bring in and out of their young life story.

This process then continues throughout adulthood. In fact, a vibrant life is characterized by a life-long commitment to the creative writing and re-writing of our life stories. Throughout life we continue to make major choices about our life script, integrating and adapting all that we have learned, and modifying our script to give it our own unique voice as we go along. Here we see again the connection between identifying and strengthening unique voice and expressing a satisfying sense of vocation in our lives.

So how is the story/movie of your life going these days? Are you excited or bored by it? Are you content or frustrated? Whatever you may be feeling, the good news is that the movie of your life has not yet been released in the theaters, because it's not finished yet! Your story is still being written. Are you unhappy in an important relationship in your life? Are you unhappy in your work? Have you lost a sense of purpose or meaning in your life? If so, that is a good indicator that it may be time to consider expanding and rewriting your script rather than passively continuing to act out a role that is not fulfilling. We cannot write a new beginning to the stories of our lives, but we can begin writing a new ending and a new next chapter today.

There are many compasses competing to guide our lives, whether we are fully aware of them or not. The same thing can be said about the many stories competing to inform our lives. The stories and beliefs we have learned from our families of origin, faith community, friends, culture, and work are primary contributors to the script of our lives. While these beliefs are influential, we must always remember that each of us, to some degree, has the power and freedom to decide and create the scripts for our lives.

The important qualifying phrase in the preceding sentence is "to some degree." The degree to which individuals have the power to rewrite the scripts of their lives is directly related to the amount of power and privilege they have in life. People who are marginalized, people without power and privilege in our culture, have limited freedom to write new scripts for their lives. The Christian story asks, in fact demands, that people of power and privilege do all in their power to create a society where everyone has equal freedom, power, and access to rewriting the scripts of their lives.

As a priest I frequently meet with people who are going through a hard time, especially a time of sudden change or loss. I am often asked some version of, "Well what should I/we do now?" While I might have some general ideas, I also know that no one else can answer such a question for them. So, my response to such a question is usually to assure them that, while their life has been completely altered by the loss they are experiencing, they will be able, with God's help, to adjust the script and write a new future beyond what they had previously imagined. Any of us who have lived more than a few decades already know the process of altering our scripts in response to unexpected changes in our lives as life is full of opportunities to adapt to change.

Our freedom to write the scripts of our lives is one of the greatest gifts we have been given. It is also one of the greatest gifts that we can work to provide for others who may currently have little freedom to write a new story for their lives. And remember that the greatest award for a well-written, and well-lived life, is not an Oscar, but rather the peace and joy that come to our loved ones and us when we dare to dream and create such a life.

▶ **Thought**

As you look back over your life, what role has your faith had in influencing the story of your life? Would you like it to play more of a role going forward?

If there were to be a movie of your life and you had to cast the leading role, who would you choose, and why? What might the title of this movie be?

▶ **Word**

Sometimes we can reflect back to one conversation, or a series of conversations, that profoundly influenced the scripts of our lives. Was there such a conversation in your life?

If you want to change or adapt your life story going forward, you will probably need to talk with others to help you do this. Is there anyone that comes to mind that you would like to talk with about this?

▶ **Deed**

Have you ever written a story, or even a few paragraphs, about your life, or about an important experience in your life? Might you consider trying that and sharing it with someone you trust?

Is there a change you want to make in your life based on your reaction to this reflection?

Reflection 4

The Many Kinds of Voice Lessons and Teachers

The King's Speech is one of the best movies I have ever seen. This movie, released in 2010, is the story of King George VI's struggle to overcome a life-long speech impediment, as he becomes king of England following his older brother's sudden abdication of the throne. The fact that this all takes place as the world is preparing for a second world war, and at the same time that radio is becoming a primary means for leaders to communicate with their people, creates a keen urgency for King George VI to face and overcome his problem with stammering. The movie culminates with King George making his first radio broadcast in 1939 to read Britain's declaration of war on Germany.

This movie is the story of an intense and powerful relationship between King George and his voice teacher/therapist Lionel Logue as they struggle together to help him find his voice, both literally and figuratively. King

George works with his teacher to overcome his stammer as he also works to discover and develop his voice as the new leader of England. King George's story is unique, and yet as I watched the movie I found myself identifying with what I think is a universal challenge: the discovering and developing of one's voice.

Having a clear voice involves much more than just the physical dimension of our speaking. It involves every aspect of who we are—our heart, soul, mind, and body. Having a clear voice means that we know what we believe and stand for and that we are able to express ourselves in a manner that is clear, passionate, and affirming. When our voice is clear and strong we stand *for* something, not merely *against* something, and we speak from the depths of our being, affirming what we know to be true.

While King George suffered from a literal speech impediment, there are other ways in which any of us also suffer from speech impediments. Whenever we are uncomfortable or hesitant to speak up we may ourselves be experiencing a form of speech impediment. I know I struggled with this when I was first ordained a pastor.

I was just twenty-five when I was ordained to the ministry. I was young, fresh out of my graduate seminary education, and I thought I knew it all. The world and church were just waiting for me to come along and enlighten them. An important part of ordained ministry is preaching and from the beginning I loved this part of ministry. Looking back on my early years of preaching however, I can now see that I suffered from a different kind of speech impediment.

My early sermons were really more intellectual treatises than sermons. I researched and wrote every word of my sermon manuscripts carefully. I edited and rewrote them repeatedly, thinking people would surely be hanging on every great theological insight that these sermons contained. I quoted extensively from religious scholars, sometimes including three or four extensive quotes in the text of the sermon. And because I spent so much time researching and writing these perfectly honed manuscripts, I was careful to read them word for word to the congregation. I shudder now to think how dreadfully boring these sermons must have been to those who had to listen. If anyone from the first churches I served is reading this, I hereby apologize for that speech impediment of mine!

Why do I say that I had a speech impediment in my early sermons? Because I now see that my overly intellectual approach to preaching was a defense against revealing anything personal or vulnerable about myself. I was hiding behind the role of "expert," rather than seeing myself as a fellow traveler, one who also has struggles and doubts on this spiritual journey we call life. In my early years as a preacher I had an impediment. While I could share how faith had touched and transformed my thinking—my mind—I was blocked in my ability to speak the truths of how faith had touched and transformed my heart and soul, how faith had transformed me and my relationships.

Things are different now, but I did not grow and mature as a preacher on my own. Quite to the contrary, actually. Along the way, I have been blessed to have colleagues and mentors from whom I learned a more personal and heartfelt manner of preaching. Gradually, over time, I have learned from them. Sometimes I asked for and they gave me explicit feedback, but most often I simply learned by watching and experiencing them in action. While I was not literally learning to sing from these colleagues and mentors, they were nonetheless my voice teachers. Over the years they have provided invaluable lessons to help me find and develop my more authentic and meaningful voice. In fact, one of the wisest observations an older colleague shared with me was that I had quoted so many experts in my early sermons because I had not yet developed my own voice and so I was trying to borrow others'. I didn't like what he was saying at first, but upon further reflection I knew that he was right. His telling me the truth about my preaching helped set me free to risk finding my own voice.

Who have been significant voice teachers for you in the past? Who are your voice teachers today? What lessons did you learn from them? These are the people who help you not merely to imitate their voices, but to develop your own voice. Parents are voice teachers—if a parent yells a lot, should we be surprised that the child grows up to do the same? Grandparents are voice teachers, and so are aunts and uncles, and other extended family members. Pastors, teachers, and coaches are voice teachers as well.

Each of us has the ability to be a voice teacher. While we may think of particular jobs or roles as lending themselves more to influencing others, a broader understanding of vocation recognizes that every one of us has the ability to offer voice lessons to the people in our lives. Each of us has the capacity to be voice teachers. To fully realize our capacity to be voice teachers, we might have to overcome an impediment within our thinking that says something like, "Who, me? Voice teachers are people like kings and queens and famous leaders. What do I have to teach someone else?"

I take great inspiration from King George VI, his teacher Lionel Logue, and how the two of them worked so intensely together to overcome King George's speech impediment. I am inspired, as I hope you are, because they show us again the importance of finding our own voices, and helping others to do the same. Each of us has a unique God-given voice that is ours alone to discover, develop, and then use to speak to the world. As we do this, we may find ourselves stammering and unsure at times, thinking that perhaps it's easier to "play small" and remain quiet, or just overly intellectualize everything, as I did in my early years as a preacher. When these self-doubts arise, we can take solace knowing the story of England's King George VI who overcame a speech disorder and self-doubt and in the process found his true voice and his true vocation.

▶ Thought

What thoughts or feelings does this reflection raise for you?

Do you think of yourself as "voice teacher" in any way? Has anyone helped you find your voice? If so, how, and with whom?

▶ Word

Are you aware of people who have been important voice teachers in your life? If it is possible, what do you think about talking to them about this and thanking them for what they have taught you?

This reflection talks about the many different kinds of speech impediments that we can encounter within ourselves. Are you aware of any "speech impediments" within yourself? Would you be willing to talk about these with someone you trust?

▶ Deed

When you look back over your life, do you see some important ways in which your voice has changed and matured?

Do you have any desire to seek out a "voice teacher" right now for some new "voice lessons"? This teacher could be a coach, spiritual director, pastor, therapist, or any friend that you trust and respect.

Reflection 5

Go With the Flow

There is something about watching a live performance that just draws me in, whether it is a concert, a sporting event, a play, or improv comedy. I admire all of the preparation and practice that has gone on behind the scenes to make the performance come to life. I respect the discipline and sacrifice that was required to make the performance a success. I don't think of worship as performance, but the live aspect of worship means that it shares some of the same dynamics and that draws me in as well.

One of the magical moments that often happens in live performances is when you get to witness one of the performers in a state of "flow." Flow is the effortlessness people feel when they are fully immersed in an energized focus so that their thoughts and emotions are fully channeled and aligned with the task at hand. When a person experiences flow their performance rises to a whole other level. Flow is when a golfer has a streak of seven straight birdies and comes from five shots back to win a major tournament. Flow is when a group of jazz musicians are improvising and creating such chemistry between their various instruments that they seem surprised by what is happening. Flow is when a performer delivers her lines or sings a song in a way that gives you goose bumps. This state of flow is also referred to as being "in the zone." When a basketball player makes ten straight shots, he or she is described as being in the zone.

The only thing better than watching someone in the flow is to experience that state in ourselves. Flow is not just for athletes or actors, it is an experience we can all have from time to time in our relationships, our work, and our daily lives. There is a certain mystical, spiritual quality to flow because we cannot make it happen at will. The term "flow" is used because there is a sense of being part of a force or energy larger than oneself, as if being carried by the flow of a river or a current of air. People experiencing this feel as if they are in the flow of something bigger than themselves.

As a person of faith, I believe that flow is in large part the movement of the Spirit in our lives; it is what makes us feel fully alive. When our efforts and will align fully with the Spirit, there is a good chance we will experience flow. This alignment, this experience of flow, can be experienced anywhere. One of the ways we know we are experiencing this sense of flow is that time passes very quickly. Have you ever had the experience of a day or an evening passing so quickly that you were surprised to see what time it was? That is because you were experiencing flow. There was something special about the activity you were doing and/or the company you were enjoying that made the time pass so effortlessly.

Flow is an unexpected gift. It is impossible to simply create flow whenever we feel like it. While it is a gift, I do believe that there are things to help maximize our chances of experiencing flow. When we focus on the following practices, we are opening ourselves to experiencing flow for ourselves and with others:

◆ Allowing ourselves to be completely in the present moment (not rehashing the past or worrying about the future);

◆ Focusing our attention on others and being curious;

◆ Living from a place of "soul" rather than ego;

◆ Participating for intrinsic value rather than trying to please others;

◆ Detaching from the outcome of what we are doing;

◆ Not forcing or trying to control an outcome;

◆ Not taking ourselves too seriously—lack of self-consciousness;

◆ Possessing a sense of humor—living lightly;

◆ Living from the "inside, out," rather than the "outside, in";

◆ Silencing our inner judge, our inner critic.

The Opposite of Flow

Distractions and being constricted block the possibility of achieving flow. This is why we use the term "choke" when a person, team, or group tightens up and performs poorly in a key situation. It is impossible to experience flow when we are distracted or when other things in our lives are out of balance. If we are constricted in other areas of our lives, that constriction will show up in our performance. I believe this is why the golfer Tiger Woods struggled for quite a while after his personal and marital crisis. Nothing changed for him physically, but everything had changed for him mentally and emotionally and therefore he struggled to experience flow again.

In many sports, when a person or team is pressing or choking or just not playing well, the coach can call a time-out to enable the individual or team to regroup. The idea of a timeout is a great idea for us as well. When we find ourselves distracted or constricted, and realize that we are pressing or choking, it is a good time to call a time-out and to regroup. Resolving distractions and then re-centering ourselves, focusing all of our attention and energy in the "now," will maximize our chances of experiencing a state of flow again.

Review the practices listed above and try putting them into action in some concrete situations in your life. Instead of being distracted, work on being fully present in a conversation with a friend or loved one. Do you experience a different kind of flow in the conversation? Try doing a task at work or home in a fully focused, mindful way and see if the task feels different to you. Try a spiritual practice of prayer, meditation, walking, deep breathing, or journaling and see if, over time, you experience more flow.

A story is told of a young man who went to see a wise spiritual teacher to ask her what she thought God wanted him to do with his life. She listened for a while, and then said to the young man, "Whatever it is that makes you feel most fully alive—do that, because the world needs more people who are fully alive."

Whenever we are true to ourselves and are using our God given talents in a way that makes the world a better place, we have a chance of obtaining that feeling we call flow. And, the more people who are experiencing flow, the better off we will all be. So what makes *you* feel most fully alive? Do that, and you will find yourself both experiencing and expressing your sense of vocation in the world.

▶ Thought

What thoughts or feelings does this reflection raise for you?

Have you experienced a sense of flow in your life? How did it feel?

▶ Word

Who is an inspiration to you? Would you say they are fully alive? How can you tell? You may want to write about this person in your journal.

When do you feel fully alive? How can you have more of that in your life? Would it be helpful to discuss this with anyone in particular?

▶ Deed

When you thought about times that you experienced a sense of flow in your life, were you doing anything differently at those times? What were the circumstances? How did it happen?

Flow is a gift and we cannot simply make it happen, but there are some things that we can do to maximize our chances for experiencing this feeling of being fully alive. What can you do to more fully open yourself to the experience of flow?

Chapter 5

ORGANIZATION

Assessing How You Organize Your Time, Money, and Possessions

My wife and I love to go canoe camping, spending a week depending only on the few things we can carry in our backpacks. When we return home after an extended camping trip we are shocked to rediscover how much stuff we own. In fact, we often wonder, "Do we own all this stuff or does it own us?" Our possessions say a lot about who we are. How we organize and take care of them also says a lot about who we are. The same is true when it comes to time and money. How we relate to and organize our time, money, and possessions is crucial to our sense of wellness. Organization is one of the eight areas of wellness of the Living Compass, and I invite you to complete the Organization self-assessment now, using the form provided in the appendix or online. When you are finished, transfer your number to the Organization wedge of the compass tool on page 155.

How Disorganization Leads to Dis-ease
Imagine you are visiting a new church for the first time and arrive a few minutes before the service. An usher greets you, but she cannot find a service bulletin to give you. She finally finds one, but when you sit down in your pew you realize it is a bulletin from last Sunday's service. The organist and choir are running behind so the service starts ten minutes late. When you look to find a hymnal to sing the opening hymn, you realize that all the hymnals are missing from your pew. The pastor, when it is time for the sermon, begins by apologizing that he had a very busy week and did not have the time to put together much of a sermon. The rest of the liturgy is equally chaotic and when the deacon says at the end of the service, "Go in

63

peace to love and serve the Lord," you realize that peace is the last thing you are feeling.

What is true about that imaginary service is also true about our lives: disorganization creates a feeling of "dis-ease." Sometimes it is hard to know which is the cause and which is the effect. Does "dis-ease" in our life create disorganization, or is it the other way around? Truthfully, one creates the other and the relationship can quickly grow into a vicious cycle. While most of us would not settle for a church that was as disorganized as the one we just imagined, we too often settle for disorganization in our own lives. We often do not realize the amount of "dis-ease" this is causing us.

As with all the areas of wellness on the Compass, organization affects and is affected by each of the other areas. This is a lesson I learned when I coached youth soccer as my kids were growing up. It was not just a coincidence that the kids who were chronically late for practice and games or who showed up without their full uniform were the same kids who were struggling with other parts of life as well. I knew this because the kids would tell me. Offering to pick kids up or calling them on a regular basis to remind them when our games and practices were happening was helpful. I was happy to do it and they were happy for the extra help, but this experience was a lesson that disorganization is related to many other aspects of our life.

Teachers and employers know this to be true as well. The student or employee who has trouble getting to school or work on time is communicating by his behavior that something is going on in the rest of his or her life. It is highly likely that if there is trouble in any other part of our life it will affect the organizational part of the Compass. When is a person most likely to make bad or impulsive decisions regarding finances? When some other area of their life is out of balance. On occasion I hear the term "retail therapy," which is a supposedly humorous description of a person making financial decisions based on emotional or relational or spiritual struggles. Instead I'm afraid it is a description of someone trying to compensate for unhappiness in another part of his or her life.

Remember that we have affirmed that spirituality is not just one area of wellness that appears on the Living Compass, but rather spirituality forms the foundation, the roots, for all the other areas of wellness. Ideally, spirituality is the compass that guides our decisions and choices in all the other areas of wellness. So how does spirituality serve as the foundation or compass when it comes to organizing our time, money, and possessions?

Even a cursory reading of the New Testament will reveal that Jesus, along with the writers of the letters in the New Testament, had a great deal to say about people's relationship with both money and possessions. It may surprise you that the Bible has some important words about our relationship with time, as well. Here are few passages.

No one can serve two masters; for a slave will either hate the one and love the other, or be devoted to the one and despise the other. You cannot serve God and wealth. (Matthew 6:24)

Sell your possessions, and give alms. Make purses for yourselves that do not wear out, an unfailing treasure in heaven, where no thief comes near and no moth destroys. For where your treasure is, there your heart will be also. (Luke 12:33–34)

Conduct yourselves wisely toward outsiders, making the most of the time. (Colossians 4:5)

For the love of money is a root of all kinds of evil, and in their eagerness to be rich some have wandered away from the faith and pierced themselves with many pains. (1 Timothy 6:10)

Wealth hastily gotten will dwindle, but those who gather little by little will increase it. (Proverbs 13:11)

These verses make it clear that there is a strong connection between our spirituality and how we relate to money, possessions, and time.

▶ Thought

What thoughts and feelings did the Organization self-assessment raise for you? You might want to write some of them down in your journal.

This reflection talks about a strong connection between spirituality and the way we organize possessions, time, and money. How do you see this connection in our own life?

▶ Word

Who or what has most influenced your attitudes about money and material possessions?

Are you comfortable talking with others about money and possessions and your relationship with them?

▶ Deed

If actions speak louder than words, what do your actions say about the importance of time, money, and possessions in your life?

As you begin reflecting on how you relate to and organize time, money, and possessions, are there any behaviors you might want to change in this area of your life?

Organizing Your Time

A story is told of a monk who had many people coming to him daily to learn from his wisdom. As a monk, he centered his life in prayer and meditation. His spiritual discipline was to start each day by sitting quietly, praying and meditating, for thirty minutes. One day a newspaper reporter was writing an article about this monk. She asked him about his spiritual discipline of daily time for prayer and meditation and he explained that this practice provided the foundation for the entire rest of his day. He said that no matter how busy his day was, he found that he had the strength and clarity to get through it because of the time he had spent that morning in silence. The reporter, knowing how busy this monk's life was with all of his responsibilities, pushed him a little and asked, "But on those days when you just have so much to do and so many people who want to connect with you, do you still make time for thirty minutes of prayer and meditation? Or on those really busy days do you sometimes skip your spiritual practice?" The monk answered without hesitation, "Oh, on those really, really busy days? On those days I awake a half hour earlier and meditate for a full hour!"

This monk knew something very important about managing time. He knew that the more demands there were on his time and energy, the more he needed to make time to strengthen his spiritual and emotional wellness. He also probably knew that all of his time was a gift from God and that paying attention to God was a way of giving thanks to God. In addition to this offering of gratitude, prayer and meditation provided the strength to meet the demands on his time and energy.

Taking more time to be prayerful when one is stressed and pressured probably seems counterintuitive and is certainly countercultural. The reporter's supposition that the monk would skip prayers when he was in a rush, perhaps reflecting choices she might make in her own life, may reflect our choices and tendencies, as well. It takes commitment to prioritize how we spend our time.

There are countless books, articles, and blogs written about time management. This fact alone tells us that time management is a challenge for many people. It is indeed a fascinating contradiction that for the last fifty years we have seen the invention of so many timesaving devices, and yet most people feel like they are more pressed for time than ever. So in the context of this retreat, I am not going to offer one more reflection on effective time management, but rather an invitation to reflect on how your spirituality influences the way you manage your time. As we continue to think about spirituality as our compass, we need to think now about what it means for it to orient the decisions we make regarding how we spend our time.

Focusing on effective time management certainly helps us to be more efficient and to complete more tasks. No one can argue that this is helpful. A spiritual approach to managing and organizing our time, however, focuses less on completing more tasks, but rather focuses on what tasks we choose to complete, and *how* we complete those tasks, paying attention to our gratitude for the gift of time.

When Our "To Do" List Connects With Our "To Be" List

It seems that telling people how busy we are has become a badge of honor in our culture. I consistently hear parents say that they regret that their children's lives are so overscheduled and busy. If these same adults were to look in the mirror, perhaps they would see that their children's overscheduled lives mirror their own frenetic ones. It seems that we have the tendency increasingly to define ourselves by what we do, how much we do, and how well we do it. Many of us seem to think that life is about being involved in everything, regardless of whether or not the activities are life-giving to us or to our families. We all can forget that less can sometimes be more.

While most people report that they are worn out by how busy they are, I find that this is not just caused by how much or what we are doing; most significantly, it is caused by what we are *not* doing.

It seems that what most busy people are *not* doing is taking time to care for their souls. We noted earlier the importance of taking time to "sharpen your saw." When people are driven to "cut down more trees" at a faster and faster pace, they tend to neglect to care for themselves—they neglect their soul-care—and in the process their "saws" become dull.

The third chapter of the book of Ecclesiastes, written some three thousand years ago, reminds us that "for everything there is a season, and a time for every matter under heaven: a time to be born, and a time to die; a time to plant, and a time to pluck up what is planted; . . . a time to keep silence, and a time to speak" (Ecclesiastes 3:1–2, 7). All spiritual traditions speak to the importance of developing a rhythm and balance in life. The primary goal of time management from a spiritual perspective is to maintain a healthy rhythm and balance in life, while keeping in mind the blessing that time is to us.

I think there is great wisdom to be learned from noting the difference between success and joy as it may help us think more clearly about how we want to spend our time. Success comes from our doing. Joy comes from our being. The ideal is for the things we do to flow out of our being, and for those same things to be aligned with who we want to be. The more our being and our doing are integrated, the more we will experience wholeness and well-being in our lives, and the more we will experience joy. Jesus desires joy for us, as he said: "I have said these things to you so that my joy may be in you, and that your joy may be complete" (John 15:11).

In this retreat we have already talked about the importance of paying attention to what we pay attention to. This is a perfect summation of a spiritual approach to time management. Pay attention to who you give your time to. Are your choices in alignment with your values? Pay attention to warning signs that may be asking you to rethink how you spend your time.

The warning signs that you are not managing your time in a life-giving way may be exhaustion, irritability, sickness, or signs of increased stress such as strained relationships. Those negative signs are God's whispers to you that things are out of balance in terms of your use of time. It is always best to listen to whispers while they are still faint rather than waiting until they turn into a shout or a crisis.

Energy Gainers, Energy Drainers

Our ideal state of being is openness to experience the joy and delight of being alive. Yet, there can often be times when we feel run down and worn out, not feeling this joy and delight. We all have activities and relationships that give us energy as well as activities and relationships that take our energy. Life is a constant flow of giving and receiving energy.

Whenever you are feeling that your energy is chronically drained, listen to the whisper and take an honest look at how you have been thinking, feeling, and acting. You will likely find a belief, habit, or even a relationship that is strained and is not healthy or life-giving. Maybe you believe that you have to be perfect at everything you do, or perhaps you have been bending over backward to please others. Maybe you simply have too much on your plate right now. Or there may also be people or situations in your life that are draining your energy. Once you get clarity regarding the root cause of your exhaustion, you can work to weed it out and better direct your flow of energy going forward. In time, you might notice that the reasons you feel run down have less to do with how much you are doing and more to do with the fact that in your heart and soul you would benefit from doing things differently. Making a concerted effort to listen to what your heart and soul really needs and desires—and then working to make it a reality—can be life-giving.

In the church, we use the word "discernment" to describe this process of thinking about what feels right in our heart and soul. When you discern who you are called to be, and then make decisions that are in alignment with that discernment, you will find that you have more energy and that your energy lasts much longer. It is wise to be aware of the effect our activities and relationships are having on our energy and then to choose wisely about how we invest both our time and our energy.

▶ Thought

Does the monk's solution to spend more time in prayer when he is
stressed make sense to you? Do you see a connection between
your spirituality and how you spend your time?

Do you find yourself thinking there just isn't enough time to get
everything done in your life? If so, how might you change your
thinking to help you resolve this dilemma?

▶ Word

Do you know someone who seems to manage time well? Would a
conversation with that person, or someone else, to talk about
how he or she manages that balance be helpful?

When you listen to yourself talk about how busy you are, or how
you manage your time, what do you hear yourself saying? Are
you satisfied with that?

▶ Deed

Many people take a passive approach to time management, acting
as if they have very little control over their schedules and time
commitments. If you feel like this, what might you do to
change this situation?

What is one small change you could make that would improve the
way you are currently organizing and managing your time?

Reflection 3

Your Relationship With Money

A joke is told of a man who was having trouble sleeping at night because
he felt so guilty about cheating when filing his taxes. He had cheated the
government out of $2,000 by underreporting income from his small busi-
ness. He felt so guilty about what he had done that he had not been able
to get a good night's sleep since filing. Not knowing what to do, he went
to talk to his priest. He confessed his wrongdoing and asked her what she
thought he should do. Without hesitation, the priest praised him for his
confession of wrongdoing and then told him that he should send a letter
immediately to the IRS apologizing for his wrongdoing and including a
check for the taxes he owed.

The man went home, thought about it for a while, and then decided on
a compromise. He decided to send the following anonymous note to the
IRS: "I am sorry to say that I underpaid my taxes by $2,000 on my most

recent income tax filing, and since that time I have not been able to get a good night's sleep. I feel horribly guilty, and so I have enclosed $1,000 in cash with this note. If I find that I still can't sleep, I will send the other $1,000 right away."

Our relationship with money is complex. We want to have the right relationship and yet, as this joke reveals, there can be a potential conflict between our own self-interest and what we know is ethical and right. There are few things in life that attract as much energy and attention as money. In all my years of marriage and family counseling, conflicts over money were among the most common triggers for seeking counseling. The conflicts were not usually about money itself, of course, but about conflicting attitudes about the use and role of money in one's life.

When we talk about one's attitude toward money, we are talking again about spirituality. Our spirituality influences and directs how we think about money, how we spend it, and how much importance we give to it in our lives. Money, in and of itself, is neutral—it is not good or bad, positive or negative, secular or spiritual. It is our relationship to money that is spiritual or not, positive or not. The Bible does not say that money is bad, but rather that "the *love* of money is a root of all kinds of evil," and that in our "eagerness to be rich" we can wander away from our faith and suffer painful consequences (1 Timothy 6:10).

Apparently some things never change. These words were written two thousand years ago and yet the wisdom is still relevant. When the love of money drives us to neglect our most important relationships, and those relationships suffer, then it is safe to say that the love of money is the root of the problem. When people compromise their health on the way to accumulating wealth, then it is safe to say with the writer of 1 Timothy that "in their eagerness to be rich" they have "pierced themselves with many pains."

Stewardship and Money

When I was a full-time pastor one of my favorite things to do was ask people for money for the church and its missions. I am not joking when I say this. I really do love to raise money because it gives me a chance to have meaningful conversations with people about what they value most in life. Talking to people about money gives me immediate access to talking to them about their spirituality. As Jesus said, "Where your treasure is, there your heart will be also" (Luke 12:34). And what I have found in talking to people about their relationship with money is that it's not just their hearts that are connected to their treasure, but their souls as well.

When the church I was serving decided to enter into a major building campaign I was pleased to work with the leaders to raise the necessary money. I remember starting out the campaign by telling this story, which apparently is true.

It was a few days before Thanksgiving and a woman who loved her church was hosting her extended family for the holiday dinner. She discovered that she had a turkey in her freezer and realized that it had been there for almost a year. She called the turkey hot line to ask if this turkey was worth serving, after having been in the freezer for so long. The turkey expert replied, "You can serve it if you wish. There is no health hazard, but I'm afraid it won't taste very good at this point." Without missing a beat our woman proclaimed, "Well in that case, I'll buy a fresh turkey and donate this frozen one to my church."

As funny as this story is, it makes a somewhat difficult point for all of us. We often do not give the best of ourselves or our money to the places and people that God would want us to share with. Let's reverse the thinking in this story and, just as we want to give our best to our family and friends, let's also work to give our best to the church and other places where we see God's spirit at work.

The church, like any organization, has language that is unique to its identity. One of the words that we use in the church when we talk about money is "stewardship." To understand the meaning of this word is to gain an important insight into a spiritual attitude toward money.

A steward is a person who manages something that belongs to someone else. A steward might manage a house, a business, a piece of property, or the finances of another person. The word arose in medieval times where, under the feudal system, the lord owned the property and had all legal authority over it. The steward managed the property and had only the legal authority that had been delegated by the lord.

When thinking about being good stewards of our money, the analogy to this medieval system is clear. God is the creator and "owner" of all that is in this world, including money and material goods. God is the lord in this analogy and we are the stewards. We are called to be the stewards, the managers of the money and possessions that we have, as we are not the owners. At the conclusion of the offering, in many worship traditions the people say, "All things come from you, O Lord, and of your own have we given you." These words (from 1 Chronicles 29:14) make clear that whatever we give to God already belongs to God.

Receiving and Releasing Your Money

The spiritual breathing practice described earlier, "Receive, Release," becomes concrete if we apply it to our relationship with money. If we meditate and pray the words while thinking about our relationship with money, then we may be praying to God to *receive* the fair compensation that we are due for the work we offer the world, and at the same time praying to be able to *release* our anxiety and over-attachment to money. This simple spiritual practice can calm our spirits where money is involved and help us gain perspective and a generous heart.

Clearly, both the man who owed money to the government and the woman who planned on giving her frozen turkey to the church are still in need of practicing the "release" part of this prayer. But then again, I'm pretty sure there is plenty of room for greater spiritual maturity for all of us when it comes to how we relate to money. Reflecting and praying honestly about our thoughts, words, and actions about money is an essential part of that spiritual maturing.

▶ Thought

What thoughts and feelings does this reflection raise for you?

In what ways do you see your spirituality guiding how you relate to money? Is there any adjustment in your thinking that would bring it more in line with your spiritual understandings?

▶ Word

Talk about the significant lessons you learned about money while growing up. Who taught you these lessons and what did they teach you? Would you say that you still see money that way?

Money has a strong effect on relationships. Is there someone in your life with whom you would like to talk about how money is affecting your relationship?

▶ Deed

Are there any practices or habits you have right now regarding money that you would like to change? If so, what would you like to try to do differently?

Are you satisfied with your current level of generosity, of giving to others in your life, or would you like to do more in this area?

Reflection 4

How You Relate to Your Possessions

In the opening reflection on organization, I shared an experience that my wife and I have when we come home from a long camping trip. When we see how many possessions we have, we wonder to ourselves, "Do we own these possessions, or do they own us?" When camping (or any other experience when the normal rhythms of life change), there is an opportunity to realize how much "stuff" is unnecessary for daily life. It reminds me of a famous statement by the eighteenth-century German philosopher Immanuel Kant: "We are not rich by what we possess but by what we can do without."

I know a couple of people who recently hired "clutter coaches" to help them organize their homes and offices. The concept of a clutter coach is new to me, but it makes sense given how involved we can be in the ongoing dance with our material possessions. "Stuff" accumulates and we need to sort through, organize, and decide what we can do without. De-cluttering our lives is like exercising, though: if we only do it every once in a while, it will not produce much benefit, but if we do it on a regular basis, the rewards are enormous. Our lives will flow better, we will be more focused, and we will not waste time looking for things.

It is easy enough to recognize when our desk, email box, or calendar is cluttered with too much "stuff." We usually know what steps need to be taken to clear out this kind of clutter. (Whether we take those steps is, of course, another matter.) Clutter appears in other areas of our lives as well, often outside of our awareness. Frequently, when people go to meet with a priest, spiritual director, or therapist, they often discover that they are carrying around emotional, spiritual, or relational clutter. They may discover that they are carrying around old feelings of inadequacy, grudges from long ago, or internalized shame-based images of God.

The word "clutter" comes from the same root as the word "clot." When a desk is cluttered to the point that a person cannot work efficiently, it is as if that person's desk has a clot. The work process becomes blocked and things do not flow. The same is true when we have emotional, spiritual, or relational clutter in our lives. This clutter becomes a clot, a blockage to wellness flowing in each of the dimensions of our lives.

At a local church I recently facilitated a Living Compass small group in which four people from a nearby retirement center participated. It was great to have an intergenerational group. These four individuals were all in their mid-eighties, quite active, and living independently in their apartments. In a Living Compass group, each member chooses one thing that he or she would like to pay particular attention to during our weeks together. At first I thought it was just a coincidence, but each of the four older members of the group chose to work on the organization area of their lives.

These older members wanted to work on de-cluttering their apartments. They each reported that they had way too much "stuff," including items they had wanted to get rid of for some time. Despite their best intentions, their initial efforts to get rid of things had failed. In our third meeting, the reason they were reluctant finally came out. One by one, each of these four people shared that the reason they were "stuck" and could not get rid of things in their apartments was that the things they needed to get rid of were all connected to memories of the past. They were things that belonged to a deceased spouse or grown child, or things that reminded them of the home they used to live in. As they shared their stories and memories, the tears began to flow, and an emotional clot began to dissolve. It was only after this sharing of their grief that they were able to begin to make progress in releasing some of the material things in their apartments. This story brings me back to the question we asked earlier: "Do we own our possessions, or do they own us?" It seems to be an important question as we all continue to reflect on how our spirituality affects our relationships with our possessions.

It is my observation that the difficulty of getting rid of possessions can be a sign of unresolved grief. I witnessed this phenomenon in a church recently. A friend of mine had recently taken the call to become the pastor of a church struggling with declining membership. While I was visiting one weekend we spent time exploring the church building, and as we did, my friend and I began to notice something. In almost every part of the building there were relics of bygone days, things that had at one point probably been used regularly by the church, but clearly had not been used in a very long time. We both could not help but wonder if all of these objects were symbolic of the congregation trying to hold on to a time when things were better. Of course congregations, like any other organization, are made up of people, so we should not be surprised that they, too, have a hard time letting go of the past and the material possessions that represent it.

Respecting the past and honoring the important people and experiences that have shaped us gives us perspective and a sense of gratitude. Our possessions only become a problem if they are interfering with our living each God-given day to the fullest.

I Want It, I Need It, I Deserve It!

By now you are aware that all areas of wellness have a strong connection with our spirituality and that our spirituality can become a guiding compass for each area of wellness. When it comes to our relationship with material possessions, we can clearly see that there are many compasses that compete to guide our decisions.

There is no denying the powerful influence the compass of our consumer culture has when it comes to influencing our decisions regarding material possessions. Most parents, for example, struggle to balance what they know is best for their children and what their children, influenced by the consumer culture, feel they must have.

This childhood struggle between wants and needs may only intensify as children move into adolescence and adulthood, influenced to want more expensive things and experiences. In a sense, there is a voice within each of us that can sound like a child insisting that he have whatever he wants whenever he wants it. We adults, as well as children, are consciously and unconsciously influenced by the compass of the dominant culture to believe that our identity and self-worth is in some way connected to what we buy and possess.

I once heard a friend say, supposedly in jest, that the stages of his desire for some "thing" go something like this. First, he says to his wife, "I want it." Next, he says, "I need it." When he no longer can resist, he finally says, "I *deserve* it." The "it" here could be any consumer good that he feels he simply must have in order to be happy.

Studies have shown that once a person's basic needs are met for food, shelter, and safety, there is no significant correlation between material wealth and happiness. The fact that many of us are reluctant to believe this is proof of the influence of our dominant consumer culture telling us that happiness is linked to material possessions.

When our spirituality guides our relationship to material possessions, those possessions are put in proper perspective. The Bible helps us with this as it reminds us that the fruits of the Spirit are "love, joy, peace, patience, kindness, generosity, faithfulness, gentleness, and self-control" (Galatians 5:22–23). Two things are worth noting about this list. The first is that the last fruit mentioned is self-control, which provides direct guidance regarding our desire for more "stuff." The second is that, as far as I know, none of these spiritual fruits can be purchased for any amount of money at any store. Instead, they are obtained through living a faith-centered life day in and day out.

There are many compasses that compete to guide the decisions we make regarding the "stuff" in our lives. I invite you to reflect on how these compasses influence your own decisions.

▶ Thought

What thoughts and feelings does this reflection raise for you? Did the section about the connection between grief and holding on to things speak to you in any way?

How strongly do you think the influences of our consumer culture affect your relationship to material possessions?

▶ Word

This reflection talks about the progression of "I want it, I need it, I *deserve* it." Do you ever hear yourself saying words to this effect?

What words of advice have served you well in guiding your decisions about material possessions?

▶ Deed

Are you satisfied with the decisions you are making about the accumulation and the importance of material possessions in your life?

Is there anything you wish to do differently regarding how you make decisions in this area of your life?

Reflection 5

Organizing Your Priorities

The last three reflections considered the organization of time, money, and possessions. Each of these important areas of life also relates to our priorities.

I like to study words. I guess you could say I am an etymologist—and if you like to study words too, then you know that that's the word for someone who likes to study words! So as I turn my etymologist inclinations to study the word "priority" I discover that it is one of those wonderful words whose meaning is clearly revealed in its root. The meaning of the word "priority" is derived from the root word "prior," which means "that which comes before, or that which comes first." So when we reflect upon our priorities in life we are simply reflecting on those things that come first in our lives. If you are asked to list your priorities regarding a specific issue or decision, you are being asked to define what comes first—what is most important for you in regard to this issue or decision.

One of the themes of this retreat is that our spirituality is our foundation and comes first, shaping and guiding all the other areas of our life. Prior to our making both small and large decisions, we consider our spiritual beliefs and values. Extending this thinking to how we organize our time, our money, and our possessions, we will see that what comes first determines how we organize our priorities as our priorities guide our decisions about our time, money, and possessions.

This familiar story is the best story I know when it comes to teaching the importance of organizing our priorities. A professor took a wide-mouthed gallon jar and filled it with ten large rocks. These rocks came to the top of the jar, and when she asked the students if the jar was full, they answered, "Yes." She didn't say a word, but instead reached down into a bucket and pulled out several handfuls of gravel and added them to the jar. The gravel easily filled in some of the spaces around the larger rocks. Then she asked again if the jar was now full. This time the students were on to her and answered, "Probably not." Smiling, she reached into another bucket and scooped up several cups of sand which, despite the fact that the jar looked pretty full of rocks and gravel, she was able to pour into the jar. Finally, she took a pitcher of water and poured several cups of water into the jar. The students watched silently, thinking. When she asked the class what lesson she was trying to teach them with this demonstration, one student offered, "No matter how full your life is there is always room to add more?" The professor laughed and said, "No, that's not the lesson. The lesson is to remember to fit your biggest and most important priorities in your life first, and then everything else will fit in around them." Perhaps the reason this story has been told so many times is that we need to be reminded of the importance of priorities over and over again!

Your Top Ten List

Let's pause midway in this retreat to ask a question. *What are the top ten priorities in your life right now?* For most of us it may take a while to sort through all the priorities of life and come up with our top ten. To help you get started, here is a list of some common priorities. Of course, each of our lists will be unique and your priorities may not be listed here. Please add your top priorities if they are not listed here.

Be a good parent	Be patient
Serve others	Be compassionate
Care for my health	Be a good friend
Be a good spouse	Practice my spirituality
Exercise more	Eat healthy food
Be generous	Give to my community
Go back to school	Get a new job
Save money	Help my church prosper
Care for my parents	Be a loving grandparent
Care for the environment	Engage in healthy recreation

Now take your top ten priorities and reflect on the decisions you are making about time, money, and possessions to see if your current decisions are in alignment with your top priorities. Are the priorities that you identified as most important currently factors in your decisions about how you spend your time and your money? Are the "big rocks" in place?

We humans have a tendency to be hard on ourselves and I want to warn against this tendency during this exercise. We all struggle with getting the "big rocks" in first from time to time. The goal of this exercise is simply to help you become more aware of the decisions you are making in regard to time, money, and possessions and to reflect on whether those decisions are in keeping with your priorities. Awareness is always the first step in making a change. We cannot change or improve something if we are not aware of it.

I once preached a sermon on the Ten Commandments in which I asked people to think of the Ten Commandments as the Ten *Commitments*. I invited people to turn the commandments into active and intentional commitments. This strikes me as a good model for our top ten priorities. What if we were to turn our ten priorities into ten commitments? What if we promised to be more reflective of how our decisions about time, money, and possessions are aligned with our priorities? Like the Ten Commandments, they could serve as a clear guide to a life filled with the fruits of the Spirit, as God promises in the fifth chapter of Galatians.

We close this fifth reflection on the Organization area of the Living Compass by returning to a guiding spiritual practice that has been present throughout this retreat. That practice has to do with our attention, and the reminder to pay attention to what you pay attention to. Applying this practice to the topic of priorities, we are wise to pay attention to and focus on our priorities more than we pay attention to the many other distracting influences vying for our attention.

Paying attention to our priorities is paying attention to our spirituality because our priorities arise out of and are built upon the foundation of our spirituality. If that all sounds a little heady, then it might be easiest to remember this advice: Always remember to prioritize your priorities!

▶ Thought

Do you think others who know you, if asked to identify your top ten priorities, would come up with the same list you created? Do you think others can recognize your top priorities by the way you live your life?

Do you agree with the idea that our priorities are an expression of our spirituality? Why or why not?

▶ Word

If you did not make a list of your top ten priorities, would you consider doing that now?

Discussing your list of priorities with someone can create an interesting conversation. Is there someone with whom you would like to have such an honest discussion?

▶ Deed

Based on your thinking and discussion about your priorities, are there any decisions you want to make in your life right now?

What's one thing you have done recently that felt good because it clearly aligned with one of your top priorities?

Living Well With All Your
STRENGTH

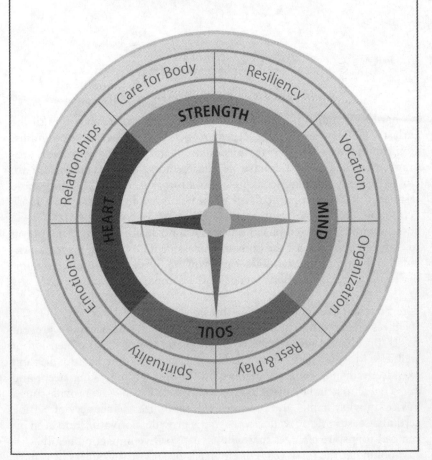

Chapter 6

CARE FOR
THE BODY

Reflection 1

Assessing Your Physical Wellness

It's hard to imagine that the word "wellness" was rarely heard until the early 1980s. Now it is heard everywhere. Schools have wellness programs. Companies have wellness programs. Retirement centers have wellness programs. Many communities have wellness centers. Wellness and health are closely related, although speaking in broad strokes, health is a more static term as it describes a particular state of being, while wellness has a more active and intentional connotation. Wellness is connected to lifestyle choices with a strong emphasis on establishing healthy habits. I invite you to complete the Care for the Body self-assessment now, using the form provided in the appendix or online. When you are finished, transfer your number to the Care for the Body wedge of the compass tool on page 155.

The Physical Dimension of Wellness
Wellness emerged as a movement in the late 1970s as a way to prevent health problems, with a primary emphasis on the physical dimension of wellness. Most wellness programs focused on promoting healthy diet and exercise, reducing tobacco, alcohol and drug use, improving sleep, and stress reduction, and many of today's wellness programs also provide sound advice on what habits and practices will minimize the chances of getting certain diseases. Many wellness programs provide motivation and even incentives to inspire changes that will have a positive impact on health.

Looking at the forty years of emphasis on physical wellness, it is hard to feel too satisfied with the progress we have made as a society. The latest projection from the American Heart Association is that Americans will be spending $800 billion annually to treat heart disease by the year 2030. Similarly, experts predict that Type II diabetes will cost Americans $500 billion annually by 2020. It is important to acknowledge that not all heart disease or diabetes is related to lifestyle choices, but much is preventable through healthier choices.

I share these statistics out of a deep concern and compassion for the suffering that is happening all around us. The intent is not to shame or judge, but to invite all of us into a more meaningful conversation to address the health problems that truly affect us all. We are in this together and we are all, in one way or another, affected by the choices that we individually are making regarding how we care for our bodies.

It is important to note that the area of the Living Compass that addresses physical wellness is called Care for the Body. We call it Care for the Body because that is exactly what we are inviting people to do in this area of wellness—to care for their bodies. Our approach to physical wellness is care-based, focusing on how we care for the amazing bodies God has created for us. The intent here is not to scare anyone, but to reflect on the wonderful possibilities intentional care offers for physical well-being.

As with all areas of wellness, our spirituality guides our decisions as we care for our bodies. As we seek to care for our bodies and our physical wellness in a kind and compassionate way, our approach is grounded in a generous and vital spirituality that affirms and celebrates the wonderful physical bodies that God has given us. Our bodies are a gift from God and we want to care for them and cherish them with love and delight. Reflect for a moment on these words from Paul's letter to the Romans:

> I appeal to you therefore, brothers and sisters, by the mercies of God, to present your bodies as a living sacrifice, holy and acceptable to God, which is your spiritual worship. Do not be conformed to this world, but be transformed by the renewing of your minds, so that you may discern what is the will of God—what is good and acceptable and perfect. (Romans 12:1–2)

There is much wisdom about caring for our bodies that we can glean from this passage. Knowing that the word "sacrifice" is related to the word "sacred," we can say that to present our bodies as a sacrifice means to present the gifts of their holy and sacred nature back to God. It is wise to remember that it is God who has given us these sacred and holy bodies in the first place.

The second part of this passage from Romans is also quite relevant to our discussion of caring for our bodies. "Do not be conformed to this world, but be transformed by the renewing of your minds" is an invitation to be counter-cultural in our approach to caring for our bodies. Given many contemporary cultural trends, that seems like good advice.

In the Book of Common Prayer there is a beautiful line in one of the Eucharistic Prayers that echo these words from scripture: "And here we offer and present unto thee, O Lord, our selves, our souls and bodies, to be a reasonable, holy, and living sacrifice unto thee" (BCP, 336).

As you reflect on your self-assessment and the remaining readings in this section of the retreat, I hope you will experience a renewed inspiration to care for the holy, wonderful gift from God that is your body.

▶ Thought

What thoughts or feelings did the Care for the Body self-assessment raise for you?

The passage from Romans talks about being "transformed by the renewing of our minds." What effect do you think your thoughts have on how you care for your body?

▶ Word

Is there someone with whom you would like to talk about the results of your self-assessment?

How we think and feel about our bodies has been shaped by the messages we were given about our bodies as we grew up. What words, what messages, did you receive about your body as a child and as a teenager?

▶ Deed

What is one way in which you currently care for your body? Is that care in alignment with what you think God would want for your body?

Is there any habit you have in caring for your body that you would like to change? What would you like to commit to doing differently?

Reflection 2

Body Language

The study of body language is the study of how people communicate non-verbal messages with their bodies. Crossed arms may signal that a person is not open to an idea that is being discussed, for example. Years ago I also learned that scratching the back of your head during a discussion often signals that you are feeling irritated or angry with the person with whom you are talking. It seems that our bodies are communicating even when we are not fully aware of this fact.

I would like to invite you to think about body language in a little different manner. Rather than just thinking about it as communicating nonverbal messages to the world, I invite you to listen to what your body may be telling you right now about your overall sense of wellness and life balance.

Our bodies always tell the truth. They never lie and are always speaking to us. Our bodies reveal a great deal about the level of stress we are experiencing in our lives. Our bodies also reveal a great deal about the day-to-day choices we are making about food, alcohol and other drugs, exercise, and sleep, and how, in general, we are caring for our bodies.

Take a moment right now and listen to what your body is telling you. Is your body feeling refreshed or exhausted? Are you feeling relaxed or tense? Is there a pain in your body that is trying to tell you something? Are you feeling weighed down or energized? Is your breathing deep and slow, or shallow and rapid?

Listening to our bodies is a good practice to develop. If we do not, we will find that the only time we listen to our bodies is when they are "shouting" at us from neglect or exhaustion. If you notice that you are feeling tired much of the time, listen to what your body is telling you. It might be telling you that you need to rebalance some things in your life. It might be telling you that you need to sleep more, exercise more, change your eating habits, and/or reduce the amount of stress you are carrying in your life. Learning to listen and respond to the "whispers" of our bodies is always preferable to waiting for our bodies to "shout" at us with more severe symptoms or disease.

I have a good friend who is newly ordained and pastors a medium-sized church. He has a real gift for pastoral care and people reach out to him for support on a regular basis. He recently told me that illness was one of the most common reasons people sought out pastoral care. This puzzled him at first. "I'm not their doctor," he said. "I wonder what they are seeking from me?" When people reach out to my friend to talk about their cancer, heart disease, depression, or other illness, they are doing so not because he is a physician for the body, but because he is a physician for the soul.

Every area of wellness is interconnected with the others. Based on this understanding, we know that what happens in one area of the Compass will always affect the other areas of the Compass. When our bodies experience disease, our hearts and souls will experience "dis-ease" as well. When our hearts and souls experience "dis-ease," we will feel it in our bodies, too. It's all interconnected by God's design.

This principle of the interconnectedness of our wellness applies to healing as well. Healing in one area of our wellness will support healing in seemingly unrelated other areas of wellness. When people seek emotional and spiritual support in the midst of dealing with cancer or any other physical illness, they are recognizing this truth. And as one involved in emotional and spiritual healing, I almost always witness a positive change in a person's physical wellness when he or she experiences healing in their heart and soul.

God Loves Every Body

What messages does our culture send to us about our bodies? What messages does our culture send to young people and teens about their bodies? What are the different messages that our culture sends to men and women about their bodies? Throughout this retreat we have been talking about the many compasses that compete to guide our decisions and choices regarding wellness in our lives. The compass of our dominant culture most certainly sends us some very unhealthy messages when it comes to caring for our bodies.

Part of the problem with the messages our culture sends us about our bodies is that they are contradictory. On the one hand we are shown standards for the male and female body that are perfectionistic, unrealistic, and not necessarily healthy. The implied message is that anyone can and should have such a body. The rates of eating disorders and the use of anabolic steroids and other performance-enhancing drugs is evidence of the harmful effects of this kind of message. Having the perfect body look is not the goal; the goal is to be healthy.

As we get messages to look a certain way, we also get messages promoting food and beverage choices that are unhealthy for us. Foods and beverages with high salt, high sugar, and high fat are constantly being marketed as though they will make us happy and satisfied. These so-called comfort foods are the very foods that end up causing a great deal of discomfort for many people, as they contribute to illnesses such as heart disease and Type II diabetes. So when it comes to body language and messages about what our ideal body should look like, my recommendation is that it all comes back to our spirituality. God designed our bodies and loves our bodies exactly as they are. God wants us to fully enjoy our bodies, and to fully enjoy them we, too, need to love and care for them so that they can be healthy and life-giving.

Loving Sexuality

In my work as a psychotherapist, the topic of sexuality comes up often. When people experience struggles in this area of their lives it is most often because they were raised with shame-based messages about their body and their sexuality. It has been my experience that many of these shame-based messages have had a religious overlay.

Sexuality is one of the great gifts that God has given us to enjoy. There needn't be anything shameful about our bodies and sexuality, as they are God-given. Our sexuality is a powerful drive and force in our lives, and as with any powerful force, I believe that God intends its use for good in our lives and in the world. Like any important force, sexuality can be used for good or for evil in our own lives and in the world. As with all dimensions of our lives, if our spirituality guides our values and is our compass with regard to our sexual life and serves as the foundation for the decisions we make, we will experience wellness in this area of our lives.

I believe that the most important spiritual truth guiding how we express our sexuality with another person is to understand that God intends for our sexuality to be connected with emotional and spiritual intimacy, and deeply knowing another person. In the Hebrew scriptures, what Christians refer to as the Old Testament, the word for sexual intimacy is translated as "to know," as in, "Adam knew Eve and she conceived." Sexual intimacy is one of the deepest ways two people can know one another and is most fully expressed when it is joined with deep emotional and spiritual intimacy. Once again, we see that all the areas of the Living Compass are interconnected. To think of sexual intimacy simply as something physical greatly diminishes it. Sexual intimacy involves and deeply expresses every aspect of our being.

God loves every body. God created sexuality and it is sacred. God loves when we treat it as such and when our bodies and our sexuality become instruments of God's joy and grace in our lives and in the world.

▶ Thought

Is there anything in particular that this reflection sparked your thinking about caring for your body? Any new ideas?

Have you ever thought about the idea that your body speaks to you? What thoughts do you have about how and what our bodies speak to us?

▶ Word

Are you comfortable talking about your body and/or your sexuality with others? Why do you think that is?

What are some of the words, some of the messages, that you hear our culture giving us (either healthy or unhealthy) regarding our bodies and our sexuality? You may want to make a list and discuss them with another.

▶ Deed

Is there a particular habit you currently have that you feel expresses a loving attitude in caring for your body?

What would like to do differently to express to God your love and gratitude for your body and its amazing capabilities?

Reflection 3

Let's Move It

Anyone who knows me knows that I have trouble sitting still. I was that kid in grade school who was always getting yelled at for tipping his chair back on two legs and rocking back and forth. And then there were always those awkward times when I would lose my balance, go crashing backward on the floor, and get that look from the teacher. I was always much better at sitting still right after gym class or recess.

This pattern has not changed substantially in my adult life. I continue to have trouble sitting still for long periods of time. I don't rock my chair back on two legs any more, but my colleagues at work can all attest to the fact that I am known to get up in the middle of a staff meeting and walk around the room as we talk.

Because of all this excess energy I have been given, I have always exercised a great deal. As a kid, of course, I didn't call it exercise, I called it having fun. I ran and played from morning to night, not because I was trying to do something good for myself, but because I couldn't resist it! I continue to run and play every chance I get as an adult, and again, it's not because I am trying to do something good for myself. I run and play whenever I can because that's how I have fun. I run and play whenever I can because that's when I feel fully alive.

I have run dozens of marathons in my life. Needless to say, I love to run. I also love to bike and play soccer. Running is not just something I enjoy for my body. It is also something I enjoy for my soul. Running is a primary spiritual discipline for me. Some of my most profound spiritual experiences and insights happen when I am running.

Please don't give me any extra credit for exercising as much as I do. I really couldn't choose to do otherwise. Like a Labrador retriever running free in a wide-open field, it's just what I do—it's how I am wired. We are all wired differently: there were kids in my class who never tipped their chairs back, as it never occurred to them to do so. There are lots of people who have no interest in running a race; they just aren't wired that way. We all, though, are designed to move and research shows that is good for our bodies to do so. We don't need to run races or play sports but it is good for all of us to be on the move, enjoying our bodies and the wondrous world around us.

Was Jesus a Runner?

Was Jesus a runner? Did Moses go to an exercise class? Did either of them ever enter a 5K race? Or did they prefer to attend a spinning or yoga class? Did they work out on a regular basis? These questions are of course silly because they are questions that could only be asked today. They obviously would not apply to the times and cultures of Jesus and Moses.

Our modern way of life is very different from that of either Jesus or Moses in many ways; for this conversation, one difference is that our life is much more sedentary. Jesus and Moses did not need to run or play soccer or attend a group fitness class because they were exercising all the time, walking almost everywhere they went. Movement and "exercise" were naturally integrated into every aspect of their daily lives without the need to sign up for classes or organized runs.

We have known for some time the health dangers of a sedentary lifestyle. In response, over the last thirty years there has been a renewed interest in physical fitness for the general public. When I ran the Chicago Marathon in 1980, for example, there were only about two thousand runners and I registered for the race the day before. When I ran the same race last year, there were nearly forty thousand runners and registration for the race sold out in six days, eight months before race day.

The latest research on our sedentary life styles reports that the negative effects of being sedentary for twenty-three hours a day does not get undone or balanced out by exercising for one hour a day; the research suggests that it is important to be moving throughout the day than rather than focusing on a specific block of time for exercise. While smoking, alcohol abuse, and obesity remain major health concerns, sitting has now also joined the list of significant health risk factors.

This latest research is captured in both the title and the content of a book by Dr. Joan Vernikos: *Sitting Kills, Moving Heals: How Simple Everyday Movement Will Prevent Pain, Illness, and Early Death—and Exercise Alone Won't.* The title says it all. Exercise is important, but everyday movement is also essential to keep our bodies healthy.

In response to this research, I recently purchased a small pedometer to keep track of how many steps I take each day, with the goal being to walk at least ten thousand steps each day. The pedometer inspires me to take the stairs more often than the elevator and to walk to places when I would normally drive. I am also linked online to a group of friends who are all using the same pedometer device and find this additionally motivating, as we can see each other's totals for any given day and week. The group connection adds fun and motivation for all of us as we work to reach our goal of ten thousand daily steps.

Churches on the Move

The power of community support to keep us moving cannot be underestimated. This is one reason that people join exercise classes, run organized races, or work with personal trainers. I am delighted to see that many churches are using their built-in ability to provide community for people in the form of fitness activities. Churches are now offering a whole range of group fitness activities. Some churches are even creating small fitness centers within their buildings. They are recognizing and celebrating the fact that the need to care for our bodies is both a physical and a spiritual need.

Walking and running groups can be one of the easiest and most effective fitness activities. Just last year I was facilitating a Living Compass wellness group at a church and two of the participants set walking goals for themselves. As they had the same goal, they decided they would meet at the church twice a week and walk together. This became the seed for a walking group that now continues at their church.

Walking groups are a wonderful example of how all the areas of our wellness are interconnected. A church walking group addresses multiple areas of wellness. The participants are caring for their bodies, developing friendships, enjoying God's creation, reducing their stress, and having fun. An added benefit of a church walking group is that it offers an opportunity for members to invite friends to join them in this church-sponsored activity.

Some churches organize seasonal walking programs such as "Walking to Bethlehem" in Advent and "Walking to Jerusalem" in Lent. In these programs the church figures out how many miles it is from either of these cities and then publicizes that number to the congregation. Members are then encouraged to walk either on their own, or as a group, and keep track of their mileage. Mileage totals are reported to the leader of the program and the weekly cumulative total for the congregation is reported each Sunday to motivate everyone to help the church reach its final goal. It's a great way to keep everyone moving, build community, and care for the bodies we have been given by God.

Churches have always helped people to discover and experience the joy that is the movement of the Spirit. Now they are also helping people discover and experience the joy that is the movement of the body. And best of all, what many people are discovering is that sometimes those are one and the same.

▶ Thought

Does the thought of exercise excite you, bore you, or exhaust you? Do you ever think of exercise as a form of play?

What do you think about the idea that regular movement throughout the day is just as important, if not more so, than exercise?

▶ Word

What messages have you been given about exercise throughout your life?

Do you talk with others about your thoughts and/or habits regarding movement and exercise?

▶ Deed

What is one way in which you currently exercise and move? If you are not exercising currently, what do you think about making that one of your new habits?

Does your church have a walking group or does it offer other physical movement activities? If not, would you consider starting something at your church?

Reflection 4

Soul Food

I recently facilitated a Living Compass small group program for parents that included both members of the host church and people from the community. In our weekly group meetings, each parent created and shared with the others a wellness goal for the coming week. The goal could be related to their spiritual, emotional, relational, physical, or vocational wellness—or some combination of these areas of wellness that would benefit them in their role as a parent.

In this particular group, one of the parents wanted to initiate the practice of saying grace as a family before dinner each night. It was clear that she was committed to this wellness goal and so we all looked forward to hearing how the adoption of this new ritual would go for her and her family. When she came back to the group the following week, she was a bit embarrassed, but because she felt safe with the group, she told us exactly what had happened. She reported that for four of the previous seven nights dinner had consisted of a trip through the drive-through of a fast food restaurant, and that the other three nights, with everyone going in different directions, the family never even sat down together to eat at the same time. The awareness was a surprise for her.

This mom laughed as she said, "It's pretty awkward trying to say grace in the drive-through when everyone's grabbing for their burgers and fries!" She added that it was also impossible to say grace when everyone was going in different directions at meal time. She realized that before she could start a habit of saying grace before dinner, she needed to become more mindful of her family's mealtime habits.

Over the remainder of our small group program, this mom set and reached a goal of Sunday night dinners with everyone in the family present and everything electronic turned off and put aside. Not only did these Sunday night dinners start with someone saying grace, but everyone pitched in and made the intentionally healthy meal together, making the whole event extra special for all.

This woman's story is not unique. It is easy for any of us to fall into less-than-ideal habits regarding how and what we eat. I am sure this woman did not create a plan to eat fast food four nights a week; it just happened in the midst of the busyness of schedules and obligations. In order to reorient the way she and her family were eating their meals, she needed to become more mindful about the choices they were all making.

Making our spirituality our guiding compass when it comes to our relationship with food can include being more mindful about how we grow, buy, prepare, and consume our food. Our bodies are designed by God to be fueled by the healthy and natural foods that God has created. If you put bad fuel into a car's gas tank, it will sputter and run sluggishly. The same is true for our bodies. They will sputter or run sluggishly if we fuel them with food that is not healthy and nutritious.

The Slow Food Movement

Are you familiar with the Slow Food movement? It began in Rome, Italy in 1986 as a local protest against the proposed construction of a fast food restaurant in a local neighborhood. In the last twenty-five years it has become an international movement. Slow Food USA, the expression of the Slow Food movement in our country, now has over 225,000 supporters. What began as a protest against the rapid spread of "fast food" has now matured into a movement that promotes and celebrates a spiritual approach to food through eating locally produced fresh fruit and vegetables, prepared at home in an unhurried manner.

My wife and I participate in a CSA (Community Supported Agriculture) program, which means that for six months each year we get our produce directly from a local farmer. The produce is delivered each week to a central pick-up point near our home, but some weeks we choose instead to drive out to the farm and pick up the produce ourselves, taking time to walk through the fields, talk with the farmers, and see exactly where and how the produce is grown. The quality and freshness of the produce we get from the farm is amazing week after week. Equally amazing has been the chance to get to know the source of the food we are eating, as it makes us more aware of the work and care real people have done to get that food to our table.

The Slow Food movement has a new parallel grassroots effort called the "Slow Family" movement. The ideas are similar—to help families find ways to reconnect with wiser ancient rhythms and rituals. Both too much fast food and too much "fast family living" are unhealthy—physically, emotionally, and spiritually. This is exactly what the woman in our Living Compass small group experienced in the way her family was eating their meals. She also learned that she could help her family create healthier, more life-giving habits by becoming more mindful of that part of their life together.

The Slow Family movement emphasizes the importance of creating relaxed, unhurried times together. Each family will have its own way of doing this, of course. Being a Slow Family may include a game night, going for a walk or bike ride together, playing in the park, cooking a meal together, going to church, or working on a service project together. It may mean an evening with no technology of any kind. Grandparents, godparents, and other extended family members can also help create an extended Slow Family by planning and participating in these slow activities.

When we slow life down, both with our food choices and our family activities, life tastes better. We sense things we would not sense otherwise. We become more conscious of the Creator of our food, and the Creator of the love and life that is in our families.

As you think about slowing down a little, be mindful that you do not try to make these changes too fast! Choose one thing you can do, one thing you want to commit to, to slow down your life, your eating, and your family.

The Church and Food

Churches and food seem to go together. Coffee hour, providing good coffee and good food each week, is often jokingly referred to as one of the sacraments of the church. Many churches also have food banks and/or meal programs. At St. Gregory of Nyssa Episcopal Church in San Francisco, for example, twelve hundred families are served free groceries each week. The groceries are placed on the altar of the church for families to pick up, reminding everyone that we can all be fed at God's table. If a church doesn't have a food bank or meal program, members of the church often volunteer at a local food bank or feeding program.

Churches have a wonderful opportunity to model healthy food choices through all the ways in which they serve food to their members and guests. For just this reason, donuts are gradually being replaced by healthier food choices at many coffee hour gatherings. There are many creative ways in which churches are connecting spirituality and food. Many churches are now becoming host sites and drop-off points for CSAs, where local farmers bring their food for purchase and pick up. Some are even offering healthy cooking classes free to the community on the day of the pick-ups, demonstrating how to use that week's seasonal produce.

Other churches are creating gardens for their members and people or groups within their local community. One church has sponsored several Karen families from southern Myanmar, in Southeast Asia. As part of helping these families settle in the United States, the church offered the families a large garden plot where families are now gardening, growing foods from their homeland that they could not otherwise find locally. The Karen families benefit from the food they grow and harvest, and the members of the church benefit as they learn about the food and traditions of the Karen families.

Another creative way that many churches are connecting faith and food is through summer Vacation Garden School programs. These programs replace the traditional Vacation Bible School and offer children and adults an opportunity to explore the connection between food and faith. Each Vacation Garden School program is unique, but most include visits to a farm or local garden or a farmer or gardener coming to speak. Plenty of opportunity is provided to dig in the dirt and to prepare and eat foods that may be new for the children. Because the Bible contains so many great stories about food, farmers, and gardening, it is easy to connect gardening and food with the stories of faith.

One other way in which churches are connecting food and faith is through what has become known as "dinner church." A group of people gather to prepare and eat a meal together, and then, still sitting at their dinner tables, the group transitions to a celebration of the Eucharist. These dinner church experiences often happen on Sunday evenings and are a prime example of how a mindful, spiritual approach to eating can positively affect our physical, spiritual, emotional, and relational wellness.

▶ Thought

Becoming more mindful about our relationship with food begins with reflecting about how we think about food. Do you think of food in a spiritual way? Do you think of food as fuel for your body or as emotional comfort?

How were your thoughts and habits about food formed? Who most influenced your thoughts about food, either positively or negatively?

▶ Word

Is there a passage, story, or parable from the Bible involving food that speaks to you? If so, what is it and what does it say to you?

If we wish to change our eating habits and become more mindful about our eating, we may need to have a conversation with family or friends about making this change. Can you think of anyone you might want or need to talk to in preparation for changing your eating habits?

▶ Deed

What habits do you currently have regarding your relationship to food that you feel good about? Is there a habit regarding your relationship with food you would like to change?

If you are a member of a church, do you think your church is making good choices that connect faith and food? How could you try to bring some of the ideas mentioned in this meditation to your church?

Reflection 5

Aging Well

When I was in high school I was invited to join a group from my church that visited skilled care retirement communities to sing with the residents. When I was first asked to do this, I must confess I was a bit hesitant. Given my own biases at that time about aging, I thought it would be really boring to spend a few hours singing with "old people." And what, I wondered, would I as a sixteen-year-old kid have in common with people in their seventies, eighties, and nineties?

I'm so glad now that I didn't give in to my discomfort, because our group's weekly visits to the retirement community eventually became an important part of my life, something I truly looked forward to each week. The delight of watching these elderly people's spirits come to life as they sang a favorite song with us was truly priceless. I was privileged to see how the gift of a visit from a friend awakens a person's soul.

I guess it shouldn't be a surprise, then, that when I served as a full-time pastor, one of my favorite parts of the job was getting to visit older folks. I felt so lucky. I mean, who gets to have visiting people with interesting stories as part of one's job? The people I most often visited were the older members of our congregation, many of whom were not able to get to church very often. It meant so much to them to have the church come to them. In fact, we had a whole team of visitors who loved visiting these folks—other people who experienced the same joy that I did in connecting with the older, long-time members of our church.

When I visited older members of our congregation, I often thought of a quotation from Abraham Lincoln, who said, "In the end, it's not the years in your life that count. It's the life in your years." Because most of the people I was visiting had already achieved a great number of years in their lives, the difference that I noticed was not the number of years they had lived, but rather the degree of life in their years. Some were still full of vitality and others were not.

Surprisingly, there was not as much correlation between a person's physical wellness and his or her vitality as I had assumed there would be. Instead, I found that those who were most vital were those who had a high degree of emotional, relational, and spiritual wellness; their physical well-being was not what made the difference in determining enthusiasm for life and their true sense of wellness.

Your Gratitude Can Make You Well

There are many stories of healing in the Bible, and quite a few of them conclude with words like this: "Go on your way, your faith has made you well." One such story is from the seventeenth chapter of Luke and involves Jesus healing ten men suffering from leprosy. In this story, ten lepers cry out to Jesus for healing, and within moments Jesus heals them and their leprosy disappears. One can only imagine their complete and utter joy as they headed to the temple to show the priests that they had been healed. As lepers, they had been judged to be unclean and thus had not been able to worship in the temple. Now that they had been healed, they must have been anxious to prove to the priests at the temple that they were healed and could therefore worship again in the temple.

The story continues and tells us that one of the ten lepers turns around before rushing off to the temple, returns to Jesus, prostrates himself at Jesus' feet, and gives thanks for his healing. Jesus wonders, "Were not ten made clean? But the other nine, where are they?" Jesus then says to the one healed man who returned to give thanks, "Get up and go on your way; your faith has made you well" (Luke 17:19).

In this story of healing, I would say that ten people were healed, but only one was made well. And what was it that made the one person well? Expressing gratitude to the One who was the source of his healing. I find that what is true for this man who was made well is also true for all of us. Gratitude, like nothing else, heals our souls and creates vitality and wellness within us and in the important relationships in our lives. Gratitude is just plain good for the soul!

A spirit of gratitude is based on humility and the generous expression of appreciation to others. The opposite of a grateful spirit is self-centeredness, or entitlement, which is rooted in a spirit of arrogance and appreciation of self. Just as leprosy was far too common in biblical times, entitlement is far too common in our world today. While leprosy disfigures the body; entitlement disfigures the soul. If we are honest with ourselves, we can all admit that we struggle with some degree of self-centeredness. This being the case, it's good to know that there is an antidote for this struggle—the practice of saying "thank you" and being truly grateful for all of life's blessings. This gratitude shifts the focus off of one's self and on to others, and on to God.

"Feeling gratitude and not expressing it is like wrapping a present and not giving it," wrote author William Arthur Ward. The practice of gratitude is distinct from the feeling or thought of gratitude. Gratitude is a habit and an attitude that has the power to permeate every aspect of our lives. Just as the power of gratitude made the one leper well, it has the power to make us and our relationships well, too.

When I visit people nearing the end of their lives, there are those to whom life is experienced as a gift and who express gratitude for that gift quite freely. Their faces shine as they share memories of what they have been blessed to experience in life. On the other hand, I sometimes visit with people who are stuck in a complaining mindset, only able to see the "half empty" aspect of their lives, focusing on the parts of life that do not seem fair. These visits always raise the question, "Which kind of a person will I be?" I also realize that I already answer that question every day by the kind of attitude and energy I choose to radiate out into the world. Every day I am aging well or not and how I look at the world in my last days will be determined by the way I live my life now.

Reconciliation

To reconcile means both to accept, and to bring into harmony or agreement. When a person accepts a difficult challenge we might say that she has reconciled herself to the fact that the way forward is going to be challenging. The other meaning is applicable when two people work through a conflict that had previously divided them. When this happens we say that they are now reconciled. Both meanings of reconciliation play key roles in aging well.

Being able to reconcile oneself to the inevitable limits and losses that come with growing older is essential for one's emotional and spiritual wellness. The third chapter of Ecclesiastes reminds us that "for everything there is a season, and a time for every matter under heaven" (Ecclesiastes 3:1). This includes times of loss and illness, as well as times of incredible blessings and joy. The same chapter from Ecclesiastes goes on to say that life is a mixture of weeping and laughing, dancing and mourning, seeking and losing, building up and breaking down. To age well we must strive to be at peace with this fact of life.

Eventually all of our bodies are going to break down. No matter how disciplined we are in our care for our bodies, they will eventually wear out. This is why it is so important for us to focus on the "building up" of our emotional, spiritual, and relational wellness throughout our life so we have the resources to face this difficult reality.

Reconciling with others and with God is of primary importance throughout life, but seems especially significant as we grow older and begin to recognize that life is too short to continue to carry resentments, especially with family and close friends. Whenever I have had the honor of helping someone face a terminal illness, one of my first questions has always been, "It there someone in your life with whom you need to reconcile right now?" Witnessing a dying person—or any one for that matter—reconnect and reconcile with a family member or friend always moves my soul.

It also moves my soul to see people reconcile and grow closer with God as they grow older. It is not a coincidence that the majority of the members of churches and faith communities are in the second half of life. It is in the second half of life, and especially in the last quarter of life, that most people think most deeply about their spiritual life and their relationship with God. If a person has been carrying an old fear-based or shame-based understanding of God for years, it is powerful to see that person begin to heal and discover a love-based experience of God as the end of life approaches. Reconciling with God after a life of human struggles and hurt, connecting deeply with the Creator, can be a significant source of strength and hope to people as they grow older.

> So if anyone is in Christ, there is a new creation: everything old has passed away; see, everything has become new! All this is from God, who reconciled us to himself through Christ, and has given us the ministry of reconciliation; that is, in Christ God was reconciling the world to himself. (2 Corinthians 5:17–19)

▶ Thought

Can you think of an older person you know, or have known, who is a role model for you, in regard to aging well? What is it about this person that makes him or her a role model for you?

What do you think about the Abraham Lincoln quotation, "In the end, it's not the years in your life that count. It's the life in your years"? Give your life some thought. Are you living in a way that will provide you with life in your later years?

▶ Word

Gratitude can be expressed in many ways, but most commonly it is expressed through the words we say to others. Do you make it a regular habit to put the gratitude you feel toward others into words?

Harsh words often divide family and friends. Sometimes the fallout from harsh words creates divisions that last for years, affecting the well-being of those involved. Finding the right words toward reconciliation can be difficult. Is there anyone in your life that you would like to begin taking steps toward reconciling with right now?

▶ Deed

What is one practice, habit, or discipline that you are doing right now that is enhancing your emotional, spiritual, or relational wellness and helping you to grow older gracefully?

Is there a new or different practice, habit, or discipline that you would like to begin to help strengthen your emotional, spiritual, or relational wellness so you are ready for the challenges of aging?

Chapter 7

STRESS
RESILIENCY

Reflection 1
***

Assessing Your Stress Resiliency

Stress can sneak up on us. It is easy to ignore or minimize the effects that chronic stress is having on us, physical or otherwise. It is even easier to ignore the effects of stress if we are surrounded by people who are also highly stressed, pushing themselves as hard as we are pushing ourselves. If everyone else on the highway is driving twenty miles an hour over the speed limit, it's less likely that we will notice if we are doing the same.

The Stress Resiliency self-assessment is designed to help you reflect on how stress may be affecting your overall health and wellness right now. Because the effects of stress can be subtle at first and easily denied, this tool is helpful as it can open up a new awareness. I invite you to complete the Stress Resiliency self-assessment now, using the form provided in the appendix or online. When you are finished, transfer your number to the Stress Resiliency wedge of the compass tool on page 155.

Developing Resiliency

In the last parish I served as rector, we had a high school student who was a committed athlete, playing soccer twelve months a year. She developed a stress fracture in her tibia, or shinbone, and described to me how the pain had come on slowly. She had ignored it and kept playing, minimizing it and thinking that it would go away, but it did not. In fact, the more she kept playing, the more painful it became, until eventually she developed the stress fracture.

Stress fractures don't usually show up on x-rays at first because they are so small, but her doctor was able to diagnosis it from the description of her pain and hearing about how hard she had been pushing herself. This young woman learned a valuable lesson about limits and not overdoing things, and was eventually able to return to playing soccer, but now making time for rest in her schedule.

Taking a closer look at some of the statements from the self-assessment will help us to more fully understand the Stress Resiliency area of the Living Compass. The first statement from the self-assessment asks us to reflect on whether there have been any major life changes in our lives over the past two years. While it is obvious that major life changes, both planned and unplanned, create stress, I am amazed at how often people either minimize this fact or do not recognize it.

Whenever I am asked to work with an individual, couple, family, or congregation experiencing some kind of distress, I always begin by asking a series of questions. One of the most important questions is whether there have been any significant changes in their lives in the last year or two. Nine out of ten times, the response is yes. They often then gradually reveal some kind of major change with which they are still very much struggling. These changes include such things as a move, a new job, a new relationship, a change in leadership, an illness or death, the loss of a job, someone leaving home, a relationship ending, financial challenges, and changes in the surrounding community where one is located. I cannot tell you how many times people have an "Aha!" moment when they come to the realization that the reason they are struggling is related to the fact that they are in the midst of a major change. This insight alone helps people become more patient with themselves and with others as they work together to address and integrate the change that is having such a large impact on their lives.

Several of the statments in the Stress Resiliency self-assessment do not refer to stress itself, but rather to how a person is responding to and managing stress. Have you ever been curious that some people seem to manage stress more effectively than others? Why is it that two people dealing with similar kinds of stress respond so differently? Why is it that one person adapts fairly easily while the other person struggles? Why is it that some people bounce back from setbacks easier and faster than others? How is it that the same stress that causes some people to collapse inspires others to rise to the challenge and grow?

The answer, in part, has to do with resiliency. Individuals, families, and organizations differ in their ability to be resilient. While some people may be blessed because resiliency comes naturally for them, the rest of us can take comfort in knowing that there are certain practices and habits that will help us to be more resilient.

A few of the habits that build resiliency are implied in the Stress Resiliency self-assessment. The first is that turning to our spiritual life can give us strength and resiliency. Remember, our spirituality is meant to function in a way similar to the root system of a tree. When our spiritual roots are strong, we will be better prepared to weather the storms of change. The challenge is that when we are in the midst of major stress and change we sometimes neglect our spiritual practices and the nurturing of our spiritual lives. Ironically, this is the very time that we need to be more intentional about caring for that root system. The importance of strengthening our spirituality on a regular basis so that its support is there for us when the storms of change arise cannot be overstated.

There is a wonderful prayer from the service of Compline that appears in the Book of Common Prayer. It speaks beautifully to turning to God for strength in the midst of change.

> Be present, O merciful God, and protect us through the hours of this night, so that we who are wearied by the changes and chances of this life may rest in your eternal changelessness; through Jesus Christ our Lord. Amen. (BCP, 133)

Another important resiliency habit suggested in the self-assessment is the support that comes from others. This includes the support that comes from a spouse, partner, friend, family member, or colleague, or from one's congregation. Just as sharing our joys with one another can greatly magnify our delight, so too, sharing our stresses with one another can greatly reduce our discomfort.

The same challenge of not letting stress negatively affect our spirituality also applies to our important relationships. Some people naturally respond to stress by isolating themselves from others, neglecting their important relationships at a time when they need those connections most. Stress can slowly sneak in and divide relationships, families, and organizations, or it can create an opportunity for people to pull closer together. We need to remain mindful and intentional about staying connected with others when we are stressed.

The last resiliency habit to highlight in this reflection is the importance of physical self-care. By physical self-care I mean eating well, exercising, and getting enough sleep. If we are not careful, changes and the stress they cause can upset each of these important functions in our lives, causing us to make poor decisions where self-care is concerned. The basics of self-care in regard to eating habits, drinking habits, exercise, and rest, are just that— basic. They are the foundation upon which we build our ability to be resilient in the midst of stress and change.

Every one of us is managing stress in our life. Like the young woman in my parish who developed the stress fracture, many of us are trying to play through pain, not taking time to rest and recover, and others are just plain tired. I hope that this and the rest of the reflections in this part of the retreat will help you to identify the signs of stress in your life, and more importantly, that they will help you to adopt or strengthen the practices and habits needed to keep you resilient and flexible amidst the changes and chances of this life.

► Thought

What thoughts or feelings did the Stress Resiliency self-assessment raise for you? Were there any surprises?

Do you think of yourself as a resilient person when it comes to dealing with stress or change? Why or why not?

► Word

Are you comfortable talking with others about your stress and worry?

Is there someone with whom you would like to talk about a stress or a change you are facing in your life?

► Deed

How do you handle the basics of physical self-care when you are stressed? How can that be challenging?

Is there a different physical self-care practice you would like to commit to?

Reflection 2

Response-Ability

Viktor Frankl, an Austrian psychiatrist, wrote a highly respected book called *Man's Search for Meaning*, about his experience surviving life in a concentration camp during World War II. The central point of this profound book is that no matter how bad things are around us, nothing can change the fact that we still have a choice about how we will respond to what is happening. "Between stimulus and response there is a space. In that space is our power to choose our response. In our response lies our growth and our freedom," says Frankl. He understood the key difference between reacting and responding. Responding, he says, is a choice, whereas reacting is something we do immediately without any conscious thought or choice.

When someone is described as "highly reactive," it is rarely, if ever, a compliment. A person who is highly reactive is someone who gets upset very easily and whose unfiltered reactions get shared with all those around him. A highly reactive person is most likely a person who is having a hard time in her life and this is how she is telling the world. Such a person can be unpleasant to be around and people may walk on eggshells around him, never knowing when he is going to be angry or grouchy. We might describe this kind of person as having a "short fuse," or a person who likes to stir up drama.

Most families, organizations, and congregations contain a few such reactive people. One congregation I served as a pastor had a few folks who were easily upset and, I now realize, were stressed and going through a rough time in their lives. This handful of people comprised less than two percent of our total congregation and yet they provided probably eighty percent of the criticism we received in the office. Most of the time it did not seem to really matter what the problem was—they had gotten into a bad habit of noticing the negative side of most everything. Almost any idea or decision that necessitated a change would bring resistance and complaints.

The challenge for each of us is to prevent highly reactive people from controlling the rest of the group, be it a family or a church. It has been my experience that most people do not like conflict, so when an angry or reactive person speaks their opinion, it is all too easy for others to remain silent. We all have seen situations in families, workplaces, and congregations where this happens: the highly reactive two percent controls the other ninety-eight percent. Needless to say, the health and vitality of any of these organizations suffers when this occurs.

I am sure you have had an occasion to deal with someone who was reactive because of other stressors. Phoebe (not her real name) was one of the founding members of the church where I was serving as the senior pastor. From what I had learned, she had been unhappy most of the last fifty years. Having recently experienced a significant loss in her family as well as some challenging health issues, she was particularly unhappy in the years that I was at the church.

Over the years Phoebe had become accustomed to getting her way. She was still in charge of several key ministries of the church, even though she was not able to function as she once had. When she complained that no one ever stepped forward to help her, other parishioners offered to help and even offered to take over if she needed to let go of these long-time responsibilities. She never realized, of course, that no one wanted to work with someone who could be as critical as she was.

I knew that I, too, was tiptoeing around Phoebe, letting her have too much negative influence. That changed one night as the congregation gathered for a final vote on the construction of a major new addition to the building. Two hundred people came together for the town hall-style meeting and everyone was invited to come forward and speak about the building project. As soon as I concluded the opening prayer and invited people to come forward, Phoebe came down the aisle, to be the first person to speak.

Not surprisingly, Phoebe spoke against the building project. What was surprising was how she chose to attack the leaders of the church, including me, blaming us for all the changes that had been happening in the church. She went so far as to say that the proposed addition was only the vestry's idea and no one else in the congregation supported it. She spoke for a good ten minutes. During the first eight minutes of her attack, I found myself wanting to react with an equally forceful counterattack. Fortunately, and by the grace of God, I was able to re-center myself and move beyond my own reactivity. As she finished speaking, I chose a response that I thought would be kind, but also not allow her to sabotage the discussion we had all gathered to have.

As soon as she finished I walked over and put my arm around Phoebe, figuring that all of her anger was not just about our plans for a new addition, but also about all the losses she was facing, including the loss of the church as she had always known it. Facing the congregation with her, I said, "I just want to thank Phoebe for getting us started in this way, because this is exactly what I was hoping would happen here tonight. My hope is that every one of you will feel free to come forward and share with us exactly how you feel about this building project. I don't want you to wait and share your feeling out in the parking lot after the meeting, I want you to come forward and share them here with everyone, just like Phoebe did." Turning to her I ended with, "Thank you, Phoebe, for setting an example for the rest of us to come forward and speak our minds. In fact, let's all give Phoebe a hand for getting this meeting off on the right foot." As the whole congregation applauded, I'm not sure Phoebe knew what to do, but she turned to me and gave me a hug before returning to her seat. I was floored and pleased.

One by one, the rest of the congregation came forward and everyone spoke their minds. They all spoke in favor of the building project and at the end of the night when the vote was taken there was only one vote against the project. Everyone left that night feeling that they had been given the chance to fully express their thoughts and feelings.

I wish I could say that I have always done a good job of responding rather than reacting. There have been more times than I would like to remember that I have chosen to be reactive rather than responsive. I know the difference between the two, though, and I know how good I feel when I am able to have the discipline to slow myself down and respond rather than react, not just at work, but in all aspects of my life.

There is a very important difference between *reacting* to stress and *responding* to stress. When we react in a negative way, we usually feel out of control, and often blame the stress, or someone or something other than ourselves, for our poor reaction. Responding is different in that it involves our being able to choose the response we wish to make. This ability to choose our response is a helpful way to think about the word "responsibility." A person with a developed sense of emotional and spiritual wellness has the capacity to slow down and create a variety of responses from which she is able to choose when she finds herself in stressful situations.

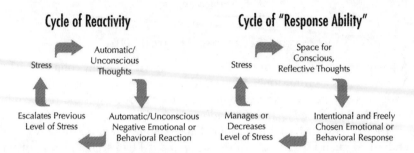

Cycle of Reactivity

Stress → Automatic/Unconscious Thoughts → Automatic/Unconscious Negative Emotional or Behavioral Reaction → Escalates Previous Level of Stress

Cycle of "Response Ability"

Stress → Space for Conscious, Reflective Thoughts → Intentional and Freely Chosen Emotional or Behavioral Response → Manages or Decreases Level of Stress

The diagram above shows the difference between reactivity and "response-ability." The tendency for any of us to react with anger or irritability when we are stressed is normal. This, however, usually results in creating even more stress. If we are able to stop ourselves and think before we speak or act, we may be able to come up with a response to the situation that could potentially even lessen the stress. It's all about being conscious and slowing down.

▶ Thought

What do you think of the Frankl passage quoted above, "Between stimulus and response there is a space. In that space is our power to choose our response. In our response lies our growth and our freedom"?

If you are emotionally reactive at times in ways that are not helpful, what are the circumstances under which that is most likely to occur? If not, how do you keep your cool?

▶ Word

Is there someone in your life whose emotional reactivity bothers you? Is your reactivity a problem for someone else?

Is it time to have a conversation with someone, either about his or her reactivity or about yours? If so, how might you start that conversation?

▶ Deed

Frankl found that "between stimulus and response there is a space." What helps you to create that space within yourself?

What practices or habits do you want to strengthen now to help you respond rather than react in the midst of stress?

Reflection 3

Living From the "Inside, Out"

A few years ago the roof of the Metrodome in Minneapolis collapsed. The Metrodome is a professional sports stadium with an inflatable roof; its collapse was caused by a heavy accumulation of snow. Until the roof could be fixed and inflated again, the stadium looked like a collapsed soufflé.

Soon after the Metrodome roof collapsed, someone came into my office and asked me if I was aware of the story and if I had seen a picture of the collapsed, inverted roof. I had. She went on to say that that picture described exactly how she was feeling at that moment. All the stress that had been accumulating in her life had finally become too heavy to handle and she was collapsing under its weight.

As we continued to meet over the following weeks she began to realize that much of the stress that had been accumulating was self-created. She realized that she had buried herself with all kinds of unrealistic, perfectionistic expectations. She also realized that she had been taking on too much responsibility for the stress in other peoples' lives. (Obviously, this is not always the case with stress in our lives.) Once she had her breakthrough insight, she began to make some different decisions, gradually re-inflating her spirit and her well-being.

When we choose to absorb the stress of others, allowing it to affect our decisions and our moods, that is living from the "outside, in." Resiliency, on the other hand, is being intentional about living from the "inside, out," creating boundaries around ourselves and our well-being and making decisions accordingly. Resiliency focuses on what we can control, on the decisions that we can make to keep ourselves well in the midst of stress. Most of us have plenty of stress to deal with in our own lives. This does not mean, however, that we are uncaring or disconnected from others. It instead means that we know our limits, aware that if we do not take care of ourselves we will become less able to care for others.

So how do we understand the common tendency to take on stress that is not our own? Is it a way to avoid our own stress? Would we rather get caught up in someone else's stress than face our own? When I think of these questions, I recall a very unusual group of people that I have been learning about recently.

Storm Chasers

It seems that many people I meet associate my hometown, Milwaukee, Wisconsin, with our cold or snowy winters, full of snowstorms that bring our activities to a standstill on occasion. Many people may not realize that Wisconsin also gets its share of tornados, averaging twenty-three such storms each year. Fortunately most of our tornados are smaller in nature and are more frightening than harmful. Of course, some tornados are fierce and when they hit dense population areas, the harm can be catastrophic.

I think it is safe to say that most of us would do just about anything to avoid an encounter with a tornado. This is true for most people, but not all. Some people, who are known as "storm chasers," do just the opposite when a tornado is near. Rather than avoiding a severe storm, these people, out of their curiosity and desire to be in the middle of the excitement, actually drive around to follow the storm, attempting to be as close as possible to its center in order to take photographs. Needless to say, this is a very high-risk activity. Over the years, storm chasers have had many close calls. It would be hard to imagine a more dangerous hobby.

I should not be completely surprised that some people love to chase storms. As a priest and a psychotherapist I have known many people who also seemed to love chasing storms. These storm chasers were of a different sort, however. They weren't chasing meteorological storms, but emotional and relational storms. It seems that some people find these personal storms exciting and are drawn to them. These storm chasers always seem to have some kind of "drama" in their lives, and they are also drawn to other people's problems, especially people who are unhappy and who have negative influences in their lives. While we certainly want to be compassionate with all people, we need to be careful of our motives. Are we truly interested in helping? Are we being invited in? Or are we merely curious and enjoy the excitement and drama?

The concept of learning to live from the "inside, out" helps us to remain resilient in the face of stress. Storm chasers, of both the meteorological and emotional type, are living from the "outside, in," allowing themselves to be caught up in others' stress on a regular basis.

Living from the "inside, out" is to chase resiliency instead. Living from the "inside, out" means making the intentional choices that will enhance our emotional, spiritual, relational, and physical well-being. It also means avoiding influences, people, and situations that will negatively affect our well-being. If we find ourselves habitually surrounded by negativity of one sort or another, it is our responsibility to become aware of our part in being connected to it—our own storm chasing, if you will. If we are getting caught up in the stress around us we need to reevaluate, making sure that our relationship to "storms" is healthy for all involved.

Of course, storms blow into all of our lives at times. Unexpected things happen and we find ourselves in the midst of an unavoidable storm. Job loss, health problems, loss of a loved one, trouble in a relationship, organizational conflict, and depression or anxiety are just some of the storms that can come into any life at any time. Given this fact, it is in my best interest to stay away from the storms and stressors that are avoidable. Besides, chasing storms can be dangerous, even deadly—not just physically, but emotionally and spiritually. That's why I, for one, will continue to try and avoid the storms I can, so that I have the energy and wellness to work through the storms that from time to time I must face.

▶ Thought

What do you think motivates a "storm chaser"?

Can you think of any ways in which you chase storms or stress in your life?

▶ Word

When people you care about are stressed and want to talk about it with you, what words of encouragement and support do you offer them?

Do you talk with others when you are stressed? If so, do you ever just "dump" your stress on them, or do you talk with them in a way that genuinely seeks their insight and perspective?

▶ Deed

Can you think about a time that you chased after or got needlessly caught up in someone else's stress storm? Why do you think that happened and how did it turn out for you?

What helps you decide what and how to help others who are experiencing a storm in their lives? Where is the healthy balance between helping others and wearing yourself out?

Reflection 4

Fight or Flight, Tend and Befriend

When we are faced with stress we can react instinctively, or we can take a breath to be thoughtful, deciding how we are going to respond. There are two different paradigms that describe how we react to stress. The first is known as "fight or flight," and the second as "tend and befriend." Thinking about each of these paradigms will be helpful as we contemplate building stress resiliency in our lives.

Fight or Flight

Imagine you are walking across the street on your way to work. Suddenly a car speeds around the corner and comes within a few feet of hitting you.

Immediately, the "fight or flight" stress response is triggered in you. Your heartbeat rises, along with your blood pressure. Your breathing becomes rapid and adrenaline floods your body. You may find yourself wanting to yell at the driver of the car as he speeds away. This reaction is completely normal and automatic. This "fight or flight" response is what helped our ancestors survive when they encountered dangerous animals or enemy tribes.

Now imagine you experience a different stressful scenario later the same morning. You are at an important meeting, and your co-worker is making veiled criticisms of your work in front of your boss. Suddenly, you find you have the urge to yell or do something physical to silence him. Your heart rate and blood pressure are rising. You are having the same stress response to this emotional threat as you had to the physical threat of the car earlier that morning. Because you have gone into the "fight or flight" mode, you are temporarily unable to talk to your co-worker or boss in a way that could be helpful.

In a previous reflection I pointed out the difference between reacting and responding to stress. We can clearly see that "fight or flight" is an extremely helpful reaction when we are in sudden danger. We sense danger and react. Thousands of years ago, in the face of a saber-toothed tiger in the weeds, survival depended on being able to respond at lightning speed. We still need this type of speedy reaction on occasion, and gratefully we have quick reflexes when danger arises. Yet while few of us encounter the life-threatening situations that our ancestors did, adrenaline-based reactions are still possible, if we are not mindful.

There are two concrete ways we can be more mindful of stress. Both involve breathing deeply when we are in the midst of stress as a way to strengthen our spiritual and emotional wellness. These are ways of building stress resiliency.

Breathing our way through stress is an ancient practice. One technique used by women in the midst of the stress of childbirth, for example, is to practice focused breathing to move through the pain. Being able to breathe in the midst of stress is an acquired skill, but one well worth practicing because it will give us the ability to create that space between stimulus and response, the space for God to enter in and calm us down before we respond.

When we talk about the importance of breathing, we can think back to the "Receive, Release" spiritual practice described in the Spirituality section of this retreat. This practice is all about slowing down our breathing. It is about breathing in and receiving God's strength and support along with breathing out and releasing our stress and worry. Doing this practice in the midst of a stressful situation is one way in which we can concretely increase our stress resiliency. I do this practice whenever I am in the midst of a stressful meeting or situation and it works every time. When I say it works,

I don't mean it magically resolves the source of my stress; instead, it increases my effectiveness in responding to the stress.

There is a second way that the "Receive, Release" breathing practice helps manage stress. When we do this practice proactively, for example at the beginning of every day, it equips us with more positive emotional and spiritual energy to face the stresses we will encounter. The state of our emotional and spiritual wellness before entering a stressful situation or conversation makes all the difference in the outcome of that situation or conversation. If I enter the situation or conversation already stressed, then I am much more likely to go into a "fight or flight" reaction and escalate the situation or conversation. If, however, I enter the situation or conversation from a place of relative calm and centeredness, then I have an increased ability to choose my responses and offer a perspective that will help resolve the stressful situation. The chance of the stress dissipating is much greater.

Tend and Befriend

A less familiar stress response model, known as "tend and befriend," is also a beneficial model for us to understand. "Tend and befriend" can shape our responses as we deal with the stressors that we encounter most often in our lives.

"Tend and befriend" is easily observable in most animals. The first part, tend, refers to the instinctual response that animals have to care for and protect themselves and their young in the face of stress. Many times while canoeing in the wilderness I have come across a family of loons or ducks, surprising them. The male duck or loon will immediately begin to fake an injury, such as a broken wing, and swim away from his family, trying to pull me away from the young birds. At the same time, the female tends to the young birds and swims away with them toward the safety of the shoreline. This behavior of tending and caring for yourself and the young in situations of danger is not unique to birds, but is evident in all of God's species.

The befriend part of the "tend and befriend" response describes the tendency of animals to seek the social support of a pack, a school, a herd, or other group as a source of safety and protection from external threat or stress. This response is helpful because predators look for an animal that has been separated from the pack or herd. Staying in close connection with the group keeps animals safe.

You and I would be wise to learn the "tend and befriend" response both as a way to prevent stress and as a very effective way to cope with it. We can apply the "tending" part of this response by recognizing the importance of tending to our own self-care and the care of those we love in the midst of stress. When we are stressed, we must be careful not to turn in on ourselves, allowing ourselves to become filled with self-doubt and self-criticism. Tending to our own self-care is a way of loving ourselves as God loves us. Tending to ourselves is to be proactive about stress and better able to cope with whatever stress we are currently experiencing.

The "befriend" part of the "tend and befriend" response is clearly good advice in helping us to be resilient in the face of stress. We humans also benefit from the protection and support provided by being part of a group. The support of a group can include that which comes from close friends, a spouse or a partner, extended family, or a group of friends. And it can include the support that comes from a congregation.

One of the things that churches do best is to provide support for its members, especially when they are experiencing some kind of upset or stress. Those of us who are members of faith communities know that sometimes we are part of the group providing support and sometimes we are the one needing that support. People turn to churches not just to find support from God, but from one another, and perhaps those two are highly related! Stress can feel like a predator sometimes, seeming to wait for just the right moment to pounce, that moment when we are vulnerable and on our own. We are wise not to get separated from the herd.

▶ Thought

Can you think of times when you have witnessed the "fight or flight" response in your life and in the lives of others you know?

Can you think of times when you have witnessed the "tend and befriend" response in your life and in the lives of others you know?

▶ Word

What are some typical words said by a person in "fight or flight" mode? What are you likely to say if you are in "fight or flight" mode?

What are some typical words said when a person is in "tend and befriend" mode? What are you likely say if you are in "tend and befriend" mode?

▶ Deed

Have you tried the "Receive, Release" practice as a way to help increase your stress resiliency? If not, would you be willing to try it? How about right now?

What helps you avoid unnecessarily going into "fight or flight" mode, when there is no real physical threat? If you do go into "fight or flight" mode, what helps you to recognize and move through it?

Reflection 5

Loosen Your Grip and Keep On Pedaling

Over the years I have learned many important life lessons from riding a bike. Recently I learned an important lesson about managing stress. At first the lesson seems like a paradox: it is possible to choose to be more relaxed while at the very same time you are experiencing greater stress.

Being something of a bike nerd, I love to read about biking. One article I read warned that many riders lose valuable energy during times of peak exertion—the very times when they can least afford the loss. The article went on to make the point that when a rider is straining his or her legs pedaling up a steep hill, there is a tendency to tense hands, arms, and upper body and to grab the handle bars with a fierce grip, thus tightening the muscles in the arms and shoulders. This tensing of the upper body does not translate into any increased output for the rider's legs, but has the opposite effect. Tension in the upper body drains energy from the lower body, where the energy is needed most.

The article went on to say that the art of riding well when a biker's legs are stressed is to keep the upper body very relaxed and loose. When I read this, I was intrigued. I wondered if it was really possible to choose to be more relaxed while feeling more stressed. I looked forward to trying out the idea the next time I was on my bike. Sure enough, I did exactly what the article had warned against. Whenever I came to a hill or tried to accelerate quickly, I immediately found myself tensing up my entire upper body—not just my arms and hands, but my teeth and all my facial muscles as well! This reaction was automatic each time I exerted myself.

I remembered the article I had read in the off-season and for the remainder of the season I tried to practice what I had read. Each time I found myself straining my legs, I worked hard to keep my hands, arms, and jaw relaxed. I consciously deepened my breathing and loosened my grip on the handlebars, relaxing my shoulders and facial muscles as well. And guess what? I could immediately feel a difference. My legs felt stronger and, most importantly, I was riding more efficiently. I could truly feel a positive difference. I learned that if I consciously took the time to relax my upper body just before I began a steep climb up a hill, the climb was much more manageable.

The application of my bike lesson to the rest of life is perhaps obvious. We all face stressors and obstacles. We all have hills, even mountains, to ride up in our lives. Like you, I have plenty of things that can be stressful in my life. Sometimes the pace of my work gets very stressful. Sometimes I have a stressful conversation with someone I care about. Sometimes I get stressed worrying about someone I love. In all of these situations, remembering to take some deep breaths and loosening my need to control the outcome of the situation has a very positive effect on how things go.

When I am about to enter a stressful situation, I take a moment to say a prayer and center myself. It always helps me to approach the situation with greater calm and greater clarity. In a sense, that's what I am also trying to do when riding my bike. I am praying that somehow I can make it up the steep hill in front of me! And because I am more relaxed I will have a better chance of making that prayer come true. Please don't take my word on all of this, though. Try it out for yourself, whether on your bike, or the next time you are about to enter a stressful situation at work or home, or when you are preparing to climb your own personal hill.

How to Boil a Frog or a Relationship

In the last section it was clear that before I could make a decision to change my biking habits, I first needed to recognize how much I was tensing and stressing my upper body. This point may seem obvious, but the problem with stress is that we often do not recognize when we are becoming stressed. And even when we begin to recognize the effects of stress in our lives, we tend to minimize those effects.

There's a story that's been around for some time about the gradual effects of stress. Whether the story is true, there is great truth in it. The story goes that there was a culture where frog meat was considered a delicacy. One day a young boy wanted to surprise his mother with a special dinner of frog. Having never prepared her favorite dinner and not having a cookbook, he did what seemed logical to him—he threw a frog into a pot of boiling water. To his dismay, the frog jumped right back out of the water and hopped out the door. While catching another frog, the boy met his mother's dear friend and told her about his problem. She told him the secret. "Place the frog into a big pot of cool water and let it enjoy swimming around. Then gradually turn up the heat. Within a matter of minutes the water will begin boiling, and the frog, not noticing the danger until it is too late, will die and you will have a wonderful dinner for your mother."

You and I are much like the frog when it comes to dealing with stress. Most of us would never choose to enter an environment that was already highly stressful. We would instinctively "jump out" immediately. It's a whole different matter, though, when stressful situations and relationships develop gradually over time.

Most relationships start out in a positive manner. But over time, any close relationship has the capacity to become heated if there is unresolved tension. If this happens gradually, it is all too easy to ignore and minimize the growing tension. Often when a couple or family comes to see me for counseling they begin with some comment like, "We wish we had decided to do this ten years ago, because there were small warning signs all along the way that we ignored." There is real danger in ignoring stress and tension in a relationship when it is first appearing. The water temperature is gradually rising and it is beginning to take a toll on us, but we are not paying attention to the change.

A relationship rarely has a sudden crisis rising out of nowhere. A crisis, instead, usually comes at the end of a long period of missed opportunities to turn down the heat and lower the tension. This is where the analogy of the frog in the water breaks down. The frog has only two choices: stay in the increasingly hot water or jump out. You and I have a third choice in our relationships and other stressful situations. We have the choice to regulate the heat, to make changes in our lives and in our relationships when we find tension heating up.

Are you in a cycle of increasing tension in an important area or relationship in your life? If so, resolve to take the third option and begin to address the situation. Begin by looking at yourself and your part in the situation or your half of the relationship. Share with the other person what you are experiencing and how committed you are to improving the relationship or situation. Ask for forgiveness for the hurt you have caused. Lowering the heat of your own internal flame will almost always influence others to do the same.

This prayer from the Book of Common Prayer serves as a reminder that quiet prayer can save us and restore our strength and confidence as we face the stresses of the world.

> O God of peace, who has taught us that in returning and rest we shall be saved, in quietness and in confidence shall be our strength: By the might of your Spirit lift us, we pray, to your presence, where we may be still and know that you are God; through Jesus Christ our Lord. Amen. (BCP, 832)

▶ Thought

One of the points made in this reflection is that it is possible for us to be stressed and not recognize its effects. Do you think this is true? Has this ever been true in your life?

The first part of the reflection talks about choosing to relax in the midst of stressful situations. The reflection talks about doing this while riding a bike. Can you think of a time when you could do or have done this in your own life?

▶ Word

What are some common words likely to cause a conversation to become heated and stressful?

When a conversation with someone you care about is heating up, what can you say to cool it down so that the conversation can be more productive?

▶ Deed

Can you think of a time in your life when you acted like the frog and did not realize until much later how much stress had gradually been heating up in your life? What do you learn from reflecting on this time?

Is there something you would like to try right now to help lower stress and/or strengthen your resiliency in the face of stress? Might regularly saying the prayer above be helpful?

Living Well With All Your
HEART

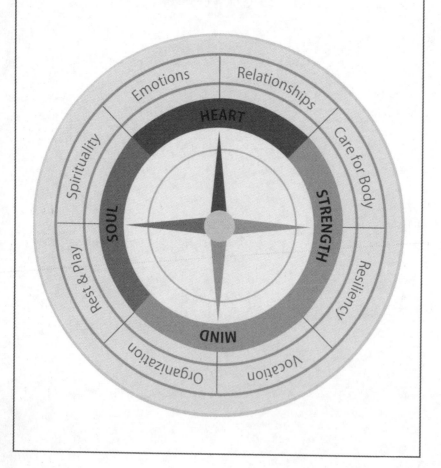

Chapter 8

RELATIONSHIPS

Reflection 1

Assessing Your Relationship Wellness

There are few things more precious in life than the loving relationships we have with others. Few things affect the quality of our life more than the quality of our relationships. We are created to be in relationship with one another and there is a powerful connection between our personal wellness and the health of our relationships. Tending to our overall personal wellness will enhance our ability to create wellness in our relationships, while creating healthy relationships enhances our overall personal wellness. And when we experience stress or anxiety in our personal wellness, this stress or anxiety will affect our relationships. The reverse is also true, of course, as stress or anxiety in our relationships will likely affect the level of stress or anxiety in other areas of our wellness.

Everyone knows the benefits that come from working proactively on one's physical wellness. When people work out, they will have greater strength, greater flexibility, and an overall greater sense of well-being. The same is true when it comes to working proactively on our relationships: we will have greater strength, greater flexibility, and an overall greater sense of well-being in our life.

The good news is that everyone can learn skills that will improve the quality of their relationships. Too often, people feel as if their relationships happen to them. The reality is that we co-create all of our relationships. Good relationships do not just happen, any more than good health happens. Both require an ongoing commitment of time and energy to making positive choices. With a new mind-set and new skills, any relationship can be improved.

I invite you to complete the Relationships self-assessment now, using the form provided in the appendix or online. When you are finished, transfer your number to the Relationships wedge of the compass tool on page 155.

The Leg Bone's Connected to the Knee Bone

There's a beautiful African American spiritual called "Dem Bones." It is based on Ezekiel 37:1–14, a well-known passage about the valley of the dry bones. Here is a portion of the lyrics:

> Toe bone connected to the foot bone
> Foot bone connected to the ankle bone
> Ankle bone connected to the leg bone
> Leg bone connected to the knee bone....

As we reflect on the Relationships area in this part of the retreat, it is helpful to see how this area of the Compass relates and connects to each of the other areas.

First, let's reflect on the Handling Emotions area found in the Heart point of the Compass. Emotional wellness—how we handle our emotions—clearly affects our relationships. If a person is having difficulty managing her anger, for example, this will affect her closest relationships. If a person is feeling overwhelmed with anxiety, this will no doubt spill over into his relationships as well. This pattern of cause and effect flows the other way, as well. If there is unresolved anger or anxiety in a person's relationships, for example, there will be a direct effect on his or her emotional wellness.

When we look at the Soul point of the Living Compass, which includes Spirituality and Rest and Play, we can see how these areas of wellness interconnect with Relationships. At the core of Christian spirituality is how one relates to one's neighbor, whether that neighbor be a family member, colleague, or a person in one's community. When we think about Rest and Play, we see that there is a natural connection between recreation and being well with others.

The Mind point of the Living Compass includes Vocation and Organization. When a person has a sense of wellness in these two areas, that wellness will naturally radiate out positively and affect one's relationships. On the other hand, if a person is disorganized with her time and finances, or dissatisfied in his work or life purpose, it will likely have a negative impact on his or her relationships.

The Strength point of the Living Compass focuses on Care for the Body and Stress Resiliency. Anyone who has had a friend or family member experience an illness or injury knows firsthand how one's physical state affects one's relationships. At the same time, the person whose physical state is compromised knows how important the support of others is in recuperation. Stress Resiliency is also highly connected to Relationships. Both affect the other, in positive and negative ways.

This quick move around the Compass shows how much our relationships are affected by all other areas of wellness, and at the same time how strongly our relationships affect our wellness in every way. I am convinced that this is a very important concept to understand. Few things affect the quality of our lives more than the quality of our relationships.

It would be hard for me to imagine ever conducting a counseling session where some relationship in that person's life is not discussed. It is also true that the other dimensions of their life are affecting their relationships. One of my tasks is to help them see that the problems they are having with other people may result from the stresses in other areas of their life. This awareness can be a source of great relief and hope. Knowing that they can work with others to adjust the stress often feels like a weight off their shoulders.

Another insight is understanding that we co-create every important relationship in our life. Relationships don't just happen. We form our relationships and then our relationships form us. We build our relationships just as we build anything else of importance in our lives. Learning new skills will help us become better builders, empowering us to create the loving relationships we and God desire.

My hope is that these five reflections about relational wellness will have a positive effect on the quality of the relationships in your life. I hope they will spark some thoughts, words, and deeds regarding your relationships with family, friends, colleagues, and neighbors. As in all parts of this retreat, I invite you to share your thoughts, words, and deeds with others. And since this part of the retreat is all about relationships, it seems especially appropriate to share this part of the retreat with others.

▶ **Thought**

What thoughts and feelings did the Relationships self-assessment raise for you?

What do you think about the concept that "few things affect the quality of our lives more than the quality of our relationships"?

▶ **Word**

There are certain people in our lives with whom conversations just seem to flow naturally. Who do you find it easiest to converse with?

Is there anyone in your life with whom you would like to have better communication? Who might that be and how would you like the communication to change?

▶ **Deed**

What is one thing you do to nurture and strengthen the important relationships in your life?

Is there anything more you would like to do to improve the important relationships in your life?

Reflection 2

Standing in Love

One of the most popular subjects for books and movies is love. There are over one million book titles with the word "love" in them and most movies have love woven in somewhere. We all have our favorite love stories, whether they be in book or movie form. Most of these favorites focus on the initial stage of a relationship, the stage of falling in love.

It's quite understandable that movies would focus heavily on the falling in love stage of a relationship, as there is great passion and drama in that part of a relationship, and passion and drama make for great cinema. The only downside to all the attention given to the falling in love stage of a relationship is that it can lead one to think that those kind of dramatic feelings are the most important part of the relationship.

Now don't get me wrong I'm all for the feelings that come with love, both the falling in love feelings and the more mature feelings of love that emerge as a relationship endures over time. Falling in love is one of the most wonderful feelings in the world, and it is a feeling not limited to romantic relationships. We can fall in love with a child, a new friend, a city, a church, a place, a job, or just about anything or anyone who means a great deal to us.

As important as falling in love is, I am even more intrigued by the idea of "standing in love." Standing in love focuses on more than just the feelings of love, referring instead to the mature commitment that emerges as a relationship endures over time. This concept is helpful because the feelings of love in any relationship can ebb and flow, even in steady, loving, long-term relationships. To reflect on what it means to stand in love is to reflect on what gives us a rock, a foundation, on which to stand in the midst of the ebbs and flows of the feelings of love.

Love Is a Decision

While we have already established that love is a very strong feeling, it is clearly more than that. Love is not just a feeling of the heart; it is also a decision of the will and of the mind. An exhausted parent who lovingly cares for a sick child or an older person who becomes a caregiver to his aging spouse is making a decision to be loving even when at times they may not feel loving. A teacher who patiently works with his most difficult students and a leader who works to mentor and develop her most difficult employees rather than firing them are demonstrating that love is a decision.

> Love is patient; love is kind; love is not envious or boastful or arrogant or rude. It does not insist on its own way; it is not irritable or resentful; it does not rejoice in wrongdoing, but rejoices in the truth. It bears all things, believes all things, hopes all things, endures all things. (1 Corinthians 13:4–7)

These words from the first letter to the Corinthians, some of the most beautiful words ever written about love, are not about falling in love, or even about the feeling of love. This description of love refers instead to a series of decisions we can choose to make. We can decide to be patient and kind. We can decide not to be irritable or rude. We can decide to endure and to believe. These are decisions that we make. They are acts of the will.

Showing patience and kindness, bearing all things, believing all things, and enduring all things are clearly ideals for any relationship, not just romantic ones. For example, these attributes describe how Mother Teresa treated the poor and the sick that she cared for. These attributes from 1 Corinthians describe the ideals for how to treat a friend, or a neighbor, or an aging relative, or a child. They are ideals for how to start a feeding program in your church as well as for how to strengthen a marriage.

Love as a decision is clear in the vows many couples make when they marry. The wedding vows in the Book of Common Prayer include these words: "to have and to hold from this day forward, for better for worse, for richer for poorer, in sickness and in health, to love and to cherish, until we are parted by death. This is my solemn vow" (BCP, 427). These vows express the core values and beliefs of commitment and perseverance. They are not based in feelings, but in a decision, a vow, to act in a certain way over time. The vows that parents and godparents make at baptism also express a decision and commitment to act in a certain way over the long term, over the course of the life of the one being baptized.

Spirituality and Love

References to 1 Corinthians 13 and Mother Teresa probably make it clear that I see a strong connection between love and spirituality. As I have mentioned many times, our spirituality serves as the compass that guides our thoughts, words, and deeds when it comes to the decisions we make about all aspects of our wellness. Our faith is clearly the primary compass that guides us best when it comes to creating and sustaining loving relationships.

For Christians, Jesus and his teachings are our compass for how to live in loving relationship with one another. Jesus taught a great deal about standing in love. He certainly acknowledged the feelings of love, but was most clear about offering us a way to stand in love. For example, can you imagine Jesus saying, "Act lovingly toward others if and when you feel like it"?

In fact, what Jesus did say was just the opposite of this. "You have heard that it was said, 'You shall love your neighbor and hate your enemy.' But I say to you, Love your enemies.... For if you love those who love you, what reward do you have?" (Matthew 5:43–44, 46). It's one thing to love someone when you are feeling warm and loving feelings toward that person. It's another thing entirely to love the person when you feel anger, disgust, and contempt. While we may think of these feelings as directed toward an enemy, they also crop up within relationships with family, friends, and co-workers, and even within church congregations.

Jesus makes it clear that immature love is when we only love others who are feeling and expressing love toward us. That is an easy kind of love, but it is immature, both emotionally and spiritually. If this had been the kind of love Jesus practiced he clearly would have dumped the disciples early on in his relationship with them, as they must have disappointed him often.

The next reflection will talk more specifically about the most common reasons close relationships lose that loving feeling. For now, just let me say that we are wise to remember that feelings ebb and flow in every relationship. What remains constant is the foundation upon which a loving relationship is built, the combination of our faith, our core values and beliefs, and our character. Together, these comprise a reliable compass to guide the decisions we make in all of our relationships.

▶ **Thought**

What do you think of the idea expressed in this reflection that love is a decision rather than a feeling?

This reflection talks about making our faith, our core values, and our character the primary compass in our relationships. What other compasses or influences do you think are guiding people in the decisions they make about their important relationships?

▶ **Word**

What words of advice would you give to a young person about the keys to creating and sustaining loving relationships?

This reflection shares words about love from the Bible, the Book of Common Prayer, and other sources. What words would you use to describe the essence of love?

▶ **Deed**

Talk about a loving relationship (friend, family, spouse, partner) that has grown and matured over time. What are some specific things you have done, and what do you continue to do, to mature and grow that relationship?

Everyone has regrets about some relationship in their lives. Talk about a relationship in which you have not been able to maintain the love you would have wished. Looking back, is there anything you wish you had done differently in that relationship? Is there anything you could do to mend that relationship?

Reflection 3

Love Banishes Fear

My wife and I love to spend time in the wilderness, as we love the quiet and spiritual nourishment we experience in nature. A few years ago we were canoeing in Quetico Provincial Park in Ontario, Canada, a remote park accessible only by canoe. One day we woke early to make the decision about whether it was safe to spend the day on the water, as a storm was predicted. My wife thought we should stay put. I thought it made sense to take off and try to get to the next lake (a mile or so away) before the storm arrived. After a brief discussion, we decided to take off, hoping for the best.

We loaded up the canoe with all our packs and took off across the very large lake. Fifteen minutes later, we were in the middle of the lake when a strong thunderstorm arose. The sky became increasingly black, the wind was whipping around us, and the temperature was dropping. Soon there was lightning in the distance, and we both knew the last place we wanted to be was sitting in a canoe in the middle of a large body of water.

So what did we do? We did what any two people would do in such a situation. We began to argue and have a fight right there in the middle of the lake! The argument started when my wife began to raise her voice over the wind, saying, "I told you there was a chance of a storm and that we shouldn't have come out today!" Soon the shouting went back and forth, with me yelling, "Why aren't you paddling harder?!" "Don't paddle on the left, paddle on the right!" And then we began to debate about which point of land to head toward.

In a few minutes we agreed to stop arguing and focus on getting to shore safely. Fortunately, a while later and safely on the shore, we found our sense of humor and realized that we had not really been mad at each other, but that the approaching storm had scared us both so much that we had begun to turn against each other. The storm was the "problem" and yet in the midst of our anxiety we had temporarily made each other the "problem."

Whenever a group of people find themselves in the midst of a "storm" they are vulnerable to turning against one another rather than turning toward one another to work together. Perhaps this is one factor in understanding why politics in our country have become so negative and polarizing. In the last several years our country has suffered through a prolonged economic "storm" that has taken a toll on many individuals, families, businesses, and institutions. In the midst of a storm it is easy to turn against one another and to cast blame on the other. If we aren't careful we might hear ourselves saying, "You got us into this mess!" "We need more paddling on the left!" "No, we don't—we need more paddling on the right!" "You are heading in the wrong direction—what are you thinking?!" What's unfortunate is that these stormy times are precisely when we need to turn toward one another and work together to face the difficulty at hand.

All groups of people are vulnerable to turning against one another in the midst of adversity or hard times. This includes couples, families, organizations, work teams, sports teams, congregations, and communities as a whole. At such times we need to remember to step back and get a larger perspective. Even when people are feeling strongly divided, there is usually more that unites us than divides us. It is up to us to work to find that common ground, no matter what group we are in.

My wife and I realized something important that day in the storm. We realized how quickly and easily we could allow our fear to divide us. We realized how quickly and easily we could allow an outside force, an outside crisis to infect our relationship. Fortunately, we were able to recover and realize that the storm was the problem and not the other. We realized that we really were in that boat together and our ability to survive the storm and make it safely to shore depended on our working together—we could not let our fears divide us.

There is a profound piece of wisdom in the Bible that speaks to the relationship between love and fear: "There is no room in love for fear. Well-formed love banishes fear. Since fear is crippling, a fearful life—fear of death, fear of judgment—is one not yet fully formed in love" (1 John 4:18, *The Message*). Love is stronger than fear. Love is stronger than any fear, including the fear of death and the fear of judgment. Mature love, well-formed love, banishes fear. The challenge for all of us is that this truth can work the other way around as well, as fear can banish love. This is exactly what happened to us in the midst of that thunderstorm on a Canadian lake. The storm created fear in both of us and the fear temporarily overshadowed our love and our ability to work together as a couple.

The Righteous Brothers recorded the popular song "You've Lost That Lovin' Feelin'" in 1964. The song received a boost in 1986 when it was featured in the movie *Top Gun*. I don't think the song's popularity is only due to its catchy melody; it addresses a difficult experience that most everyone encounters at some point, whether in a romantic relationship or a relationship with a friend, colleague, or within a group. Losing that "loving feeling" in any kind of relationship is always painful.

Whenever I work with a group of people who have "lost that loving feeling," whether that group is a couple, a family, or a congregation, most often the loving feeling is being covered up by some combination of fear and anger. My work with them will usually focus on helping them to rediscover the love underneath their fear and anger. This does not mean we will not address the fear and anger; rather, it means that we will address it from a broader context of what unites the couple/family/congregation, rather than from what is currently dividing them.

I remember vividly working with a conflicted congregation. The pastor and vestry were locked in a standoff about several issues and the anger was thick in the room. After I listened to their anger for a while, I discerned that we needed to shift the energy in the room. I told them that I didn't really know much about their congregation and its history. I told them I'd heard a lot about the hurt and anger they were feeling, and now I would like to hear some stories about what they love about their church and what their church has meant to them through the years.

The first story I heard was from a woman whose husband had died two years prior. She teared up as she talked about the beautiful funeral held at the church and how she never could have made it through the last two years without the support of the congregation. A man spoke next about how much it meant to him when their church served every month at the local feeding program. A couple spoke about how all six of their children had been baptized at the church and how it had always been an anchor in their lives.

A few more people talked and when they had finished, the energy in the room had completely changed. The hearts and souls of everyone there had softened. To refer back to the canoeing story, it was as if the storm had passed and the sun had come out. There was still much work to be done—there was still a long way to paddle—but they had a much greater realization of their shared love and desire to work together.

At the beginning of the congregational meeting the members' fear had blocked their love for one another. A shift had taken place, though, after several members shared stories about the love they had experienced in their church over the years. At that point, love was stronger than the fear. The fear, along with the conflict that still needed to be worked through, was still there. The difference was that with softer hearts and loving spirits, productive conversations could be had that would help lead to compromise and resolution of the conflict.

▶ Thought

What do you think of the scripture quoted in this reflection, "There is no room in love for fear"?

What do you think of the idea that love banishes fear, but that fear can also banish love?

▶ Word

Talk about a time when fear caused you to act unkindly toward someone you love.

In addition to fear, what else can banish love or make it hard to act lovingly?

▶ Deed

When have you acted in a way that demonstrated the power of love as stronger than the power of fear? What specifically did you do to show that the power of love is stronger than the power of fear?

Is fear affecting an important relationship in your life right now? If so, what could you do to minimize its power and effect on you and that relationship?

Reflection 4

How Our Neighbors Can Teach Us About Love

One of the core teachings of the Christian faith is to love your neighbor as yourself. Many believe that the primary beneficiary of that mandate to love is our neighbor. Whenever God has called me to love a new neighbor, I am the one that ends up growing and receiving so much.

When I speak with people who have served at a meal program, worked in a homeless shelter, gone on a service trip, visited a shut-in, volunteered in a domestic violence shelter, tutored in an after-school program, or served in any kind of pastoral care ministry, they regularly say that they received as much, if not more, than they gave. Our faith becomes real when we are asked to truly know, love, and serve our neighbor. Our comfort zones are stretched when God asks us to love someone that we may have previously judged.

The Parable of the Good Samaritan is about two religious leaders—a priest and Levite—who chose to walk right by their neighbor in need, deciding not to get involved. I include the entire parable here because it is so relevant to our reflecting on being in right relationship with our neighbor.

> Just then a lawyer stood up to test Jesus. "Teacher," he said, "what must I do to inherit eternal life?" He said to him, "What is written in the law? What do you read there?" He answered, "You shall love the Lord your God with all your heart, and with all your soul, and with all your strength, and with all your mind; and your neighbor as yourself." And he said to him, "You have given the right answer; do this, and you will live." But wanting to justify himself, he asked Jesus, "And who is my neighbor?" Jesus replied, "A man was going down from Jerusalem to Jericho, and fell into the hands of robbers, who stripped him, beat him, and went away, leaving him half dead. Now by chance a priest was going down that road; and when he saw him, he passed by on the other side. So likewise a Levite, when he came to the place and saw him, passed by on the other side. But a Samaritan while traveling came near him; and when he saw him, he was moved with pity. He went to him and bandaged his wounds, having poured oil and wine on them. Then he put him on his own animal, brought him to an inn, and took care of him. The next day he took out two denarii, gave them to the innkeeper, and said, 'Take care of him; and when I come back, I will repay you whatever more you spend.' Which of these three, do you think, was a neighbor to the man who fell into the hands of the robbers?" He said, "The one who showed him mercy." Jesus said to him, "Go and do likewise." (Luke 10:25–37)

Perhaps one of the reasons that Jesus is so insistent about loving our neighbor is that he knows that in and through that interaction we will be taught a great deal about love. I suspect that the Samaritan in this story was changed by and through his interaction with the stranger he found along the side of the road—a stranger that the Good Samaritan treated not as a stranger, but as a neighbor. Sometimes God brings a person, a neighbor, into our lives because that person, that neighbor, is not just in need of our care or love, but has something very important to teach us.

The Chess Teacher

I was in New York City recently and I had some free time one sunny spring afternoon. Being an avid chess player, I walked over to observe some games being played by the locals at Washington Square Park, a place known for its gatherings of chess lovers who play at the stationary chess tables located in the park. The park's chess players are quite famous and have been featured in many movies, most notably *Searching for Bobby Fischer,* and I wanted in on the action. Playing a game of chess at Washington Park had always been on my bucket list.

As I approached the tables in the southwest corner of the park, I noticed there were several intense games going on. Many had spectators surrounding them and so I joined in to watch some high level chess, hoping to learn a thing or two. I walked around for some time, watching several games, when I heard a man call out to me. He motioned me over and asked if I wanted to play a game. I was delighted to do so. We introduced ourselves; his name was James.

James, whom I had noticed earlier while I had been watching the other games, was sitting by himself, surrounded by a few bags of what I assumed were all of his worldly possessions. Now at a chess table with all the pieces set up, he invited me to play. He graciously offered the white pieces, which if you know anything about chess, means he was giving me an advantage. I tried to defer, but he would not hear of it. He said he was a regular at the park and as I was obviously a guest, I should play the white pieces.

I'm not proud of this, but I was already making the assumption that I was going to be a much better chess player than James. I was trying to let him play white to give him the advantage that I was sure he would need. Again—and I'm embarrassed to admit this—I made the assumption that a person living on the streets probably wouldn't be very good at chess. This was the first lesson I learned, even though it's something I seem to have to learn over and over again: it is unwise to judge a person based on their appearance. How many times have we done this, and how many times have we judged wrongly? Appearances really tell us so little!

I made my first move with white, and immediately realized I had misjudged James. After I completed my opening move (a Queen's Pawn opening, for those of you who are chess players), James looked me in the eye and announced, "Now there's one more detail we have to agree on. I play all my games for ten dollars a game—winner take all." The fact that he said this confidently and with a glint in his eye confirmed for me that I was in the presence of a brilliant chess player. I continued my opening with the Queen's Gambit, one of the most popular openings in chess, which he chose to accept. He then went on to play a variation of defense that I had never seen before. I kept thinking to myself, "This man is a genius," at the same time feeling so embarrassed about how I had prejudged him.

The game went back and forth for a long time. We traded pieces every step of the way and the game was completely even for the first forty-five minutes. I was hanging on as best as I could when he made a brilliant move to capture a passed pawn I had on the far left side of the board. In a close game, the loss of one pawn can be the difference between victory and defeat, and in this case that's exactly what happened. Ten moves later James won the game by checkmating me.

I learned two important lessons during my game with James. The first is to be more aware of the filters I use as I make assumptions about my neighbor. These filters, rarely helpful, are almost always wrong. Every one of us is much more complex than what our simple appearance reveals. The second lesson I learned is this: Always be open to learning something new from your neighbor. You see, after our game ended, James took the opportunity to teach me a lesson about why it is important to advance a passed pawn early in a game. He recreated from memory the exact set-up of the board that was before him when he made the winning move. He showed me how I should have played the situation and how I could have forced a tie game if I had played my passed pawn correctly. The lesson was brilliant. For a good ten minutes he was my teacher and I was his student.

When I stood up to leave I handed James a twenty-dollar bill. He said he wasn't sure he could make change for a twenty. I said there was no need for change—that ten dollars was for his victory, and the other ten dollars was for the lesson about how to advance a passed pawn correctly. I refrained from mentioning that the more important lesson he had taught me that day about loving my neighbor was priceless.

We all have neighbors in our lives that are easier for us to judge than love. These neighbors may be in our families, workplaces, communities, or congregations. My experience with James is a reminder of how easily our filters and judgments toward others can become a log in our own eye, blocking our ability to see our neighbor as the child of God he or she truly is. It is at those moments that God, and our neighbor, have something important to teach us if we are but humble enough to learn.

▶ **Thought**

In the story of the Good Samaritan, why do you think the priest and Levite walked around and avoided getting involved with the person in need?

Can you think of a person in your life right now you are finding it hard to love? Are you aware of a judgment or a "log in your eye" that might need to be removed in order for you to love this person?

▶ **Word**

Talk about a time when you have learned something important by allowing yourself to reach out to a stranger.

Is there anyone you walk around, not wanting to help? Is there someone God is calling you to reach out to? To speak differently about? To talk with differently?

▶ **Deed**

What deeds do you do right now that express your love for your neighbor? What lessons have you learned from these deeds?

Are there other deeds that would show more fully your love and respect for your neighbors? What might you learn if you did this?

Reflection 5

Who Do You Appreciate?

When I played Little League baseball as a child, and again when I coached it as a parent, there was a wonderful cheer that we would offer after every game. Win or lose, we would gather together as a team and chant, "Two, four, six, eight, Who do we appreciate? Yeah, Tigers!" (or whatever the name of the other team was). This small, good sporting gesture is still a great reminder for me today of both the importance and the power of appreciation.

If you look up the definition of "appreciate," here is what you will find:

1. to be grateful or thankful for.
2. to value or regard highly; place a high estimate on.
3. to be fully conscious of; to be aware of.
4. to raise in value. *

---
* www.dictionary.com

When it comes to the importance and power of showing appreciation, each of these four nuances has something important to teach us.

To be grateful or thankful for: When we say to someone, "I so appreciate the effort you made for our family, team, group, or church," we are letting them know how grateful we are for what they have done. It is easy to take others for granted, and the people who mean the most to us are often the ones we take most for granted.

To value or regard highly; place a high estimate on: For example, "I appreciate a good meal, or a well-pitched baseball game." With this nuance, expressing appreciation to others says to them that what they do is valuable to us. "I really appreciate the patience you show to your aging mother" is not just expressing gratitude, but saying to the other person, "I admire and place a high value on the way in which you handle yourself."

To be fully conscious of; to be aware of: An example of this would be, "I fully appreciate the challenges involved in this situation." Being appreciative begins with a shift in consciousness and awareness. It shows that we understand the challenges that others are facing. Empathy begins with being conscious and aware of what others are feeling. What a wonderful gift we give to others when we let them know that we understand what they are going through in their lives. Saying to someone who is really stretching to help someone else "I appreciate how much you are giving of yourself right now" shows that we are conscious and aware of the sacrifice they are making.

To raise in value: For example, "This antique has appreciated a great deal over the last fifteen years." This nuance of the word is important when it comes to appreciating others; our appreciation can increase their sense of value and self-esteem.

So when I show heartfelt appreciation to someone I care about, I am doing any or all of the following: I am thanking them, I am telling them I value who they are and what they are doing, I am being conscious and aware of who they are and/or what they are doing, and I am raising their self-esteem! Two, Four, Six, Eight—Who do *you* appreciate?

The Grass Is Always Greener
We are all familiar with the saying, "The grass is always greener on the other side of the fence." When we are frustrated in a relationship, a job, or the church we attend, it is sometimes easier to think that we would be better off in a different relationship, job, or church. Many times this is not the case, however. If we go over to the "other side of the fence" we will often find that there are just as many weeds and dry patches as on the side we left behind.

I like a twist on the saying: "The grass is always greener where we water it." When we pay more attention to and truly appreciate our relationships we are, in effect, watering them. Whatever we water, whatever we pay attention to, is what grows. Remember that your results in the Living Compass Self-Assessment Tool, including the Relationships section, simply show what areas of your life you have been watering and what areas of your life are a little dry.

If a relationship in your life is a bit wilted right now, consider how you can water it with appreciation. Know that it doesn't have to cost a cent—it can be something small, like a hug or an encouraging word. When our three children were little I used to embrace them in a bear hug and squeeze them tight. Whenever I was doing this I would tell them that I was filing up their "love tank." I told them that each person is like a car, needing fuel to make them go. I would explain that cars need gas and people need love, and so while cars have gas tanks, people have love tanks, and that we need to fill up each other's love tanks whenever we can. Truly appreciating others is one way to fill up their love tank. It is also a way of watering the grass that is that relationship, remembering that grass is greener where we water it.

You Are in Love

There is something unique about the way we express ourselves when we feel love for someone. We commonly say, "I am in love with _____," filling in the blank with the name of the person we love. What is unique about this expression is the idea that we are "in" something, not that we are feeling something. We do not use this idea of being "in" something when we express other feelings. For example, we do not say, "I'm in sadness"; we say, "I'm sad." We say, "I'm happy" or "I'm angry," not "I'm in happiness" or "I'm in anger."

When we say that we are "in love," we are, perhaps without realizing it, acknowledging that we are participating in something much larger than ourselves. When we feel love for one another, no matter what form of love it may be, I believe that we are connecting with the One who is the very source of love. Each expression of our love for one another is a manifestation of the love of God, a love that is all around us, within us, and between us at every moment. It is in God's love that we live and move and have our being.

You and I are like light bulbs when it comes to loving one another. Light bulbs do not create the electricity that runs through them. They do, however, reveal the presence and power of that electricity. Just as a light bulb does not create electricity, we do not create love. Each of our loving relationships, though, is a unique expression of the electricity of love that flows throughout the universe.

We are all already *in love* whether we recognize it or not. We cannot help but exist in that love anymore than a fish can help but exist in water. We stand in the midst of God's abundant love at every moment. And because of that fact, we have the opportunity to share and radiate love in *all* of the relationships in our lives, learning not just to love our neighbors as we love ourselves, but to love and appreciate our neighbors as God loves and appreciates us.

▶ Thought

What do you think of the expression of being "in love"? Do you think of it as meaning that love comes from a power higher than yourself?

Can you think of a time in your life when you thought the grass was greener on the other side of the fence, only to find out that this was not the case?

▶ Word

Words are powerful. Most of us have had experiences when we have felt depreciated by what someone has said to us. Has this happened to you? What was said that caused you to feel depreciated? Have you ever done this to anyone else?

Think of a time when instead you truly felt appreciated by someone. What words were said that made you feel appreciated? When have you said appreciative words to someone else?

▶ Deed

Is there someone who could benefit from a show of greater appreciation from you? What might you do to show your appreciation?

Is there a relationship in your life that needs some "watering" right now to become a little greener? What might your part be to provide some of that water?

Chapter 9

HANDLING EMOTIONS

Reflection 1

Assessing Your Emotional Wellness

The writer of the book of Ecclesiastes reminds us that there is "a time to weep, and a time to laugh; a time to mourn, and a time to dance" (Ecclesiastes 3:4). In fact, not only this writer but all the writers of the Bible remind us that God is present in and through the full range of all our emotions. Every human emotion is expressed in the Bible, from ecstatic joy to debilitating despair.

Even a cursory reading of the Psalms reveals the emotions being lived and expressed by their writers. Jesus experienced and expressed the full range of emotions, including anger and feeling forsaken. Our faith does not insulate us from feelings of despair or anguish. Our faith, however, does act as a compass for us, helping us to keep our bearings in the midst of any emotional storm that we may be experiencing.

In the Relationships section of this retreat we noted that faith helps us to "stand in love" and to choose to be loving even when we may not be experiencing the feelings of love. Our faith can provide a firm foundation upon which to stand when our emotions ebb and flow. And as people of faith, we also know that our faith can be the greatest source of true joy in our lives. As Jesus said, "I've told you these things for a purpose: that my joy might be your joy, and your joy wholly mature" (John 15:11, *The Message*). Mature joy is the fruit of our faith and as this passage makes clear, it is what God truly desires for us.

I invite you to complete the Handling Emotions self-assessment now, using the form provided in the appendix or online. When you are finished, transfer your number to the Handling Emotions wedge of the compass tool on page 155. As you scale each of the statements, remember that you are simply reflecting on each of these statements as they apply to your life at this moment. If your scores are lower than you would like, remember that this simply means that this is a part of your "garden" you have not been watering and it is a bit wilted right now. This section of the retreat will help you water your emotional wellness so that the mature joy that God desires for you can more fully bloom.

Handling Our Emotions

My wife and I recently met with a church youth group to discuss the connection between faith and wellness. We began the discussion by asking the teens how they would describe someone they thought was well and how that differed from someone they thought was not well. To help facilitate the discussion, my wife drew two columns on a large piece of paper, with a line down the center. At the top of the column on the left she wrote the words "Not Well" and at the top of the column on the right side she wrote "Well."

When we asked the teens to give us words to put under each column, the first word they offered for the "Not Well" column was "cranky." The next several words were "angry," "bad mood," and "crabby." When we asked for words to put in the "Well" column, the words they offered were "happy," "laughs a lot," "energetic," and "fun to be around."

We found it fascinating that all the words that the teens provided were actually connected to emotional and spiritual wellness. No one mentioned anything about weight, exercise, or diet, for example, as we might have expected. For this group of teens, a person's state of wellness was exhibited by their emotional and spiritual wellness.

I have thought a great deal about the first response that this group of teens gave to the question, "How do you know if someone is not well?" They said that you would know because that person is *cranky*. It is such a simple observation and yet at the same time it is quite profound.

As I think about this in my own life, I realize that indeed one obvious sign that I am not well is that I become cranky. I can become cranky because I don't feel well physically. I can become cranky because I am experiencing a problem in an important relationship in my life. I can become cranky because my work is not going well. I can become cranky because I have not been tending to my spiritual life. I can become cranky if my life is disorganized. This pattern clearly shows that my emotional wellness is strongly connected to, and is strongly affected by, every other aspect of my wellness. My emotional wellness is like a thermometer, indicating that another area of my life is in need of attention.

While it is true that other areas of wellness affect our emotional wellness, it is just as true that our emotional wellness affects all other areas of our wellness. When our mood is out of sorts, it has the capacity to affect the other areas of our lives. When we feel chronically flat or tired, it cannot help but affect other areas as well. When we feel chronically cranky or angry, this, too, will have a negative effect on the rest of our lives. To minimize the potential trouble, it is wise to "read the thermometer" and make the necessary adjustments to lower the temperature.

It is important to note that the area of the Living Compass that addresses emotional wellness is actually entitled "Handling Emotions." This is important because to a large degree our emotional wellness has to do with how we handle our strong emotions. We all experience the full range of emotions and that is good and normal, as all emotions are given to us by God. Our emotional wellness has to do with the choices we make when we feel strong emotions. It has to do with how we handle and manage the emotions which ebb and flow in our lives.

Let's imagine that I have experienced a recent setback or disappointment in my life. I am feeling sad and a bit discouraged. These feelings, these emotions, are simply what I am feeling, neither good nor bad. How I choose to handle those emotions has a great deal to do with my emotional wellness and can be good or bad, helpful or not helpful. I could choose not to handle them well by becoming cranky and criticizing everyone around me. Or I could choose to handle them by isolating from others, shutting them out. On the other hand, I could choose to handle my emotions well by sharing my sadness and disappointment with others whom I trust. By choosing to acknowledge my vulnerability and sadness, I will begin to feel better and at the same time deepen and strengthen the relationships with the people with whom I am sharing my feelings.

Emotional wellness is high when we have the ability to:

- ◆ Feel and express the full range of emotions in a healthy manner.

- ◆ Adapt to change gracefully.

- ◆ Recognize when emotions are not being handled well.

- ◆ Have a variety of "tools" in our emotional tool kit that allow choices in handling emotions.

- ◆ Maintain a sense of humor, a positive outlook on life, and take ourselves less seriously.

Much has been written in recent years about emotional intelligence. It is now clear that the higher our "EQ," or emotional quotient, the greater the satisfaction we will experience in all aspects of our lives. A higher EQ is an indisputable contributor to our overall happiness. A high degree of emotional intelligence is characterized by the ability to stay calm and centered in the midst of strong emotions around us. A person with a high degree of EQ can choose her responses rather than be overtaken by a "knee jerk" reaction. While there may not be much that can be done to raise our intelligence quotient, or IQ, there is a great deal that can be done to raise our emotional quotient, or EQ. The remainder of the reflections in this part of the retreat will focus on some of the things we can do to raise our EQ.

▶ Thought

What thoughts and feelings did the self-assessment for Handling Emotions raise for you?

What do you think about the connection between our faith and our emotional wellness? This reflection included a few biblical passages that relate to emotions. Can you think of any others?

▶ Word

This reflection shared some words that a group of teens offered in response to the question of how they know if someone is well or not. If you were asked the same questions, what words would you offer about both being well and not being well?

What words from the Bible or other wisdom writings have provided guidance for you in handling your emotions?

▶ Deed

What is one thing you do in your life to enhance your emotional wellness?

Is there something you would like to add to strengthen your emotional wellness?

Reflection 2

If You're Happy and You Know It

Most of us are familiar with the children's song, "If You're Happy and You Know It." The song invites us, the singers, to express our happiness in a variety of ways, including clapping hands, stomping feet, turning around, and shouting, "Hooray!" The popularity of this song is no doubt related to the fun that people have in participating in the actions associated with being happy.

There is a simple bit of wisdom in this song that speaks to one of the primary components of emotional wellness. This song doesn't simply talk about the importance of expressing our happiness, it also provides methods of expression through the various actions and gestures. The simple wisdom in this song is that when we feel an emotion—in this case happiness—it is best to express it. When you know you are feeling something, go ahead and express it. The ability to feel and express the full spectrum of emotions in a healthy way is a key component of emotional wellness.

Imagine there is a continuum of emotions on a scale from 0 to 10. Think of the emotions on the lower end of the scale, from 0 to 5, as the "difficult or unpleasant" emotions, such as fear, worry, anger, sadness, and anxiety. Now think of the emotions on the upper end of the scale, from 6 to 10, as the "pleasurable" emotions, including joy, love, excitement, and delight. The farther you move toward either end, the more intense the emotions become. Right in the middle, at the number 5, is the neutral point where you do not really feel much of anything, pleasant or unpleasant.

Now that you have this scale in mind, I invite you to think about how it applies to your ability to feel and express your emotions. How comfortable are you with letting yourself feel and express the full range of your emotions, from being exceedingly happy to being very upset? Are you comfortable with the whole range, or do you prefer a narrower range of 3 to 7, or 4 to 6? For clarification, I am speaking about expressing emotions in healthy ways. Expressing anger through violence, for example, is not a healthy way to express anger. Talking about how very angry you are and working to solve whatever the problem is that is upsetting you, on the other hand, is healthy and productive and is an example of emotional wellness.

I remember working with a man who was having trouble creating and maintaining relationships. When I shared this emotional scale with him, he had an "Aha!" moment. When I asked him if he thought he was more of a 0 to 10 or a 3 to 7 kind of person, he didn't have to think long before he exclaimed, "I'm more like a 4.5 to 5.5 kind of person!" He explained that his first reaction whenever he felt any strong emotions was to try to contain them. After all, he told me, he didn't want things to get "out of control."

Here's an important and somewhat surprising insight. There is a strong connection between the degree to which we are comfortable feeling and expressing "unpleasant" emotions and the degree to which we feel and express "pleasurable" emotions. The man who assessed himself as being stuck in the 4.5 to 5.5 range eventually realized how limiting this had become for him. He had worked hard to shut out all of the "negative" emotions he had been feeling, leaving him unable to experience joy and other positive emotions in his own life and in his relationships.

Young children are the best example we have of comfort in expressing the full range of emotions. Observe young children at a playground for a while and you will most likely see them express every emotion imaginable. One moment they are shrieking with delight as they come down the slide, and the next moment they are sobbing loudly. A moment later they are angry at a child who will not share, and then they are hugging that same child. Eventually they will be crying with sadness as they have to go home.

There was a time when we could more comfortably express the full range of our emotions. Over time, though, we began to internalize which emotions were appropriate to express and which were not. The cultural influences that taught us these rules about expressing ourselves include our families, the schools we attended, the societal norms for our gender, the culture of our faith community, and the larger culture in which we live.

The Bible clearly contains stories of people feeling and expressing every possible emotion. Anger, lust, greed, joy, ecstasy, fear, depression, delight, sadness, discouragement, arrogance, and love are all in the Bible. They all are given to us by God as reflections of our internal states, signs that things are or are not going well. It is our responsibility to respond to those emotions by communicating them to others in a healthy way, working to find solutions to situations that cause the "negative" emotions or celebrating the "positive" ones.

An Emotional Wellness Paradox

Jesus expressed many of the great truths regarding being a Christian through the use of paradoxes. A paradox is something that on the surface seems contradictory, but in essence reveals a truth. For example, Jesus said, "Many who are first will be last, and the last will be first" (Matthew 19:30). He also said, "Whoever wants to be first must be last of all and servant of all" (Mark 9:35).

There is an important, paradoxical truth when it comes to emotional wellness: sometimes we need to be comfortable with feeling worse first in order to feel better. This is often the case for couples in counseling. Typically a couple tells me that the joy has gone out of their relationship. They report that there is a flatness to the relationship and that they feel emotionally stuck. They want to recapture the joy and excitement they once felt.

What I tell them first is not what they want to hear. I tell them that most likely their lack of joy is directly related to unexpressed anger, frustration, or sadness. I explain that if they want to feel more joy, they are first going to have to become comfortable with feeling and expressing their "negative" emotions with each other as well.

Referring back to the image of the 0 to 10 emotional continuum, a "stuck" couple is often living in an emotional range of 4 to 6. They are not experiencing the positive emotions of joy and delight, but they are also not experiencing—or more accurately perhaps, are not expressing—the "negative" emotions of frustration or hurt. In order to help this couple rediscover the joy they previously knew, I will first need to help them express the unhappiness that they are feeling. Without knowing it, this couple's decision to wall off any negative emotions has also resulted in their positive emotions being closed off. We cannot choose to wall off or mute only a portion of our emotions. What happens is that we end up muting or walling off all of our emotions. As the couple begins to risk opening up some of their anger and hurt, they may feel worse in the short term. The paradox is, though, that this feeling worse is almost always the bridge to feeling better as joy and love begin to flow again.

Have you ever had a good argument with a friend or loved one that resulted in you growing closer together? Then you have experienced this paradox. You needed to feel worse before you could feel better. The argument released your pent-up negative emotions and allowed the positive emotions to flow again.

▶ Thought

What do you think about feeling the full range of emotions? Does it seem healthy or dangerous?

What is the range of emotions that are you comfortable feeling and expressing?

▶ Word

Talk about the cultural influences of family, gender, and faith and how they have influenced how you feel and express emotions.

Is there a relationship in your life in which you would like to change the way you are expressing and handling emotions? Are you ready to have the conversation you want to have with that person? What do you want to say?

▶ Deed

Emotions are expressed not just in words, but in deeds. What are some actions that express your emotions of fear, anger, or joy?

What do you want to do differently to be more emotionally well?

Reflection 3

When We Can't Untangle Ourselves

A few years ago a beautiful story unfolded in the ocean waters just outside of the Golden Gate Bridge in California. An adult humpback whale had become entangled in numerous crab nets and traps and was struggling for survival when a fisherman saw the whale and radioed for help. The more frantically the whale tried to break free from the nets, the more it became entangled. The whale was getting weaker, to the dismay of everyone who was watching.

When help arrived it became clear that there was no way the whale was going to be able to free itself. The only possibility of saving the whale was for divers to enter the water and cut the nets off the whale. This was going to be risky, but was less dangerous than might be expected, as the whale was so exhausted.

The divers began their rescue attempt and those working near the whale's head reported that they felt the whale's eyes watching them as they slowly cut the nets. The divers' courageous efforts were successful and within a few hours the whale was free. Before swimming off, the whale circled the boats several times, seemingly expressing its gratitude to those who had saved its life.

I have been both the whale and the divers in this story at different times in my life. I have been the one in need of help and the one to give help. I'm guessing this is true for most of you as well. There have been times when I have been tangled up in worry about how I was handling a difficult situation and other times when I have been tangled in grief or self-doubt. What made the difference in each situation is a friend or loved one who took the time to listen to my worries and help me sort through them. A listening ear, and a listening heart, can help set us free, giving us the clarity we need to choose a course of action, resolve our worry, or move through grief.

I have worked with people who find themselves tangled up in shame, guilt, and self-criticism. This can result in more tangles—tangled up relationships or unintended tangles with alcohol or drugs. While the divers used knives to free the whale, the primary tool we have to help others who are ensnared is simply our loving and compassionate presence. One conversation at a time, we can help cut the cords of whatever nets are binding them.

Perhaps you know someone who is tangled up in some way right now. Maybe it is you. Any of us can get entangled in worry, grief, self-doubt, anger, an unhealthy relationship, or some kind of addiction. Perhaps the story of the helpless whale and the divers will inspire us to reach out for help when we need it or to do what we can to make a difference for another. The divers had no idea if they would be successful, yet they had the courage to try, and the whale was able to trust that the divers could help.

When Grief Entangles Us

Unresolved grief is one of the things that often tangles up a person's life. Unresolved, or what I call "frozen" grief, is often the "elephant in the room" when a person does not know why they are not feeling or doing well. Unresolved grief can affect every aspect of our wellness, creating physical, spiritual, relational, vocational, and emotional distress. And like the whale in the story, we often cannot disentangle ourselves from the nets of grief; we will need the loving presence of others to set us free.

Grief is exhausting. It drains our energy and our ability to concentrate. I once worked with a woman who was a computer programmer and who was seeking to become untangled and released from the pain of her grief. In our conversations I shared with her a metaphor of how I understand the way grief can affect our wellness, often without us even being aware of its full effect.

I asked this woman what happens when a person tries to open and run too many applications on a computer at the same time. She explained that the applications will either crash or they will run very slowly. I explained that this is how it works with grief, too. When people are experiencing acute grief, it is as if they have a powerful "application" running on the computer of their heart, mind, soul, and body. This grief "application" is using up much of the space they need to process their day-to-day lives. Any other "applications" they try to use will run slowly, perhaps crashing at times. Even if they are not actively thinking about or feeling their grief or loss, the "application" of grief is always running in the background. They never know when it will pop back up again and demand their full attention. To honor and make room for their grief, they may need to close some of the other "applications" in their lives, acknowledging the real limits that grief places on energy.

When we are grieving, we may wish that we could just close or quit this grief "application"; we yearn to be done with it and get on with the other things we need to do. It turns out, though, that there is no "force quit" for the "application" of grief. The only way to begin to untangle ourselves from the nets of grief is to talk about our grief to others who have the love and patience to listen. When people are willing to be that listening presence for us, and when we are willing to be that listening presence for others, the nets of grief will slowly become untangled and eventually we will be able to swim freely again.

These truths about grief apply not just to individuals, but to groups as well. Families grieve. Organizations grieve. Congregations grieve. Dioceses grieve. Denominations grieve. Nations grieve. When I am asked to work with a congregation experiencing some kind of difficulty, I will almost always discover the presence of unresolved or "frozen" grief. Whether it is grieving for the "good old days," the loss of a beloved lay or clergy leader, or the loss of members through death or a move, the grief is entangling their present efforts to move forward. The congregation will first need to acknowledge and work through its collective grief before it can minister to others who have had a loss in their lives.

I cannot overstate how often I find unresolved grief to be present in people's lives. That's the bad news. The good news is that in our churches we already have the most important ingredient necessary to help people heal from their grief: community. One of the most powerful healing ministries that congregations can offer is to help people heal from and untangle their grief. We cannot untangle ourselves. And in fact, even though I can provide some limited counseling support to a person who is experiencing grief, I always encourage them to find a community, a congregation, within which they can continue their healing.

If you are a member of a congregation, I invite you to think about someone you know in your church who has experienced a loss recently. The loss might be the death of a loved one, a job loss, a health crisis, a financial loss, or a natural life-stage loss of someone leaving their lives. I invite you to consider how you might be called to reach out to them and, like the divers in the story, assist them in becoming free from their grief. Reaching out to others who are entangled in grief or any other kind of emotional pain is at the heart of the gospel. As followers of Christ, we are followers of the One who came to untangle us, which it was clear that we were unable to untangle ourselves.

▶ **Thought**

This reflection speaks of grief as being the "elephant in the room" when a person or group of people are suffering. What do you think of this idea? What do you think of the idea of a congregation being affected by "frozen" or unresolved grief?

Grief can greatly reduce our ability to concentrate and think clearly. Have you ever had this experience, or know someone who has?

▶ **Word**

Talk about a time when you helped untangle someone from a loss or grief he or she was experiencing.

Talk about a time when someone helped to untangle you from a grief or loss that you were experiencing.

▶ **Deed**

What could you do to help yourself feel better when you are dealing with grief, or just feeling a little down?

If you are a member of a faith community, what does your faith community do to help people who are entangled in grief or some other kind of emotional distress?

Reflection 4

Emotional Resiliency

I love the word "resiliency." It's a fun word to say and I love the way it sounds. It sounds hopeful. Even more than how is sounds, I like what it means. To be resilient means to be able to bounce back and recover one's emotional and spiritual center in the midst of difficult conditions. Resiliency is not so much a trait a person possesses, as a skill a person can learn. There are certain habits that can be cultivated to build resiliency. We have already reflected upon this concept in the Stress Resiliency section of this retreat. Here, I want to expand that reflection and talk about resiliency as a key skill in handling our emotions and maintaining our emotional wellness.

Recently I had the joy of facilitating a conversation with forty church administrators about emotional resiliency in the workplace. As in many work settings, when there is stress in the workplace, these administrators are often the ones most affected. It doesn't matter where you work today, there are increasing challenges to maintaining emotional centeredness in the workplace as we are working longer hours or multiple jobs, taking on increased workloads, or finding it is harder than ever to keep personal time separate from work time.

Perhaps you are one who is having your emotional wellness challenged in the workplace right now. Or perhaps your emotional wellness is being challenged in your personal or family life. Whatever the nature of your stress, here are a few suggestions that emerged from the conversation I had with those wise church administrators. Their suggestions can help any of us become more emotionally resilient in the face of stress.

The first thing the administrators all agreed upon was the importance of awareness—being able to honestly recognize the early warning signs that stress is building up and becoming a problem in one's life. So before we talked about emotional resiliency, we had an honest conversation about the challenges to managing our stress and our emotional wellness in the workplace. At the workshop I asked the group, "What are the warning signs for you that your emotional wellness is becoming compromised?" Here are some of their answers:

◆ I get irritable and snap at people, either at work, or at home.

◆ I have trouble sleeping.

◆ I eat poorly, eating comfort food that's not good for me.

◆ I shut down and pull away from everyone.

◆ I get sick a lot.

◆ My allergies get much worse.

◆ I feel really anxious and have what feel like panic attacks.

◆ I cry a lot.

◆ I work more hours, but get less done because I'm tired and unfocused.

◆ I stop exercising—the very thing I need to do more!

Our group agreed that the earlier we notice these warning signs that we are stressed, the easier it is for us to make the changes or adjustments necessary to recover our emotional balance and resiliency.

Our group then went on to discuss the habits and practices that help maintain an emotional center in the midst of stress. Here are some of their responses:

- ◆ Develop and nurture one's spiritual life.

- ◆ Exercise on a regular basis. It will do as much for one's moods as for one's body.

- ◆ Create healthy boundaries. Know your limits and practice saying "no."

- ◆ Cultivate optimism. Whatever we pay attention to is what will grow.

- ◆ Create or connect with others to build a social support network. No one needs to go it alone. Resist the urge to isolate from others or to become irritable and short with them.

- ◆ Keep your sense of humor!

I have found that while all of the things on this list are important, developing and nurturing one's spiritual life is what often has the biggest effect on our emotional wellness. At the same time, I am aware that it is often the last thing most people think of trying.

There is a great deal of research now on meditation and mindfulness, and the documented positive effects they have on an overall sense of emotional well-being. Mindfulness and meditation are now being taught in medical schools and most stress management programs now incorporate some kind of mindfulness or meditation practice. While this research is helpful, it simply confirms what people of faith have known for thousands of years: prayer and meditation are not just good for the soul, but are good for the heart, mind, and body as well.

Challenges to our emotional wellness happen. They are ubiquitous these days. Emotional resiliency happens, too. The key difference is that stress happens whether we want it to or not, while emotional resiliency is something that we have to choose to make happen.

The River of Our Emotions

The word "emotion" comes from the Latin word *emovere,* which means "to move." We recognize this sense of the word when we talk about being emotionally moved by something someone said or did. To experience emotion is to be moved, to be stirred up. One way to think about the sense of movement that is implied in the word "emotion" is to think of the word as "e-motion." What I conclude from this root meaning is that emotions are meant to flow. They are meant to flow in and through us. If our emotions are meant to be in motion, then it makes sense that problems with our emotional wellness will begin when the flow of our emotions becomes blocked.

The image of a river is often used when discussing centering prayer as a way to allow and observe the free flow of our emotions. Imagine yourself standing on a bridge overlooking a river. The river is your emotions and it is always moving. As you look upstream, you realize that you can never know what will flow around the bend of the river. The image of being on the bridge and looking down on the river provides us with a perspective of observing our emotions without becoming one with them, and allows us to be more comfortable with the unknown from around the river's bend.

The most important thing to remember in this metaphor is not to jump in! If you are feeling sad, feel and observe the sadness, but let it flow through, under, and past you. If you are feeling angry or joyful or any other emotion, feel and observe the emotion, and let it flow through and past you. Our soul—our spiritual life—provides for us a bridge on which to stand and observe the flow of our emotions without becoming overwhelmed by them.

In his letter to the Ephesians, Paul makes a similar point when it comes to handling our emotions. "So then, putting away falsehood, let all of us speak the truth to our neighbors, for we are members of one another. Be angry but do not sin; do not let the sun go down on your anger" (Ephesians 4:25–26). Here Paul offers us a bridge to stand on by helping us to understand that our feelings—in this case, anger—are a natural part of who we are. It is what we do with our feelings that can potentially separate us from God. Paul makes it clear that holding on to one's anger is a sin. If we do not let our anger go before the sun goes down, as Paul advises, it is an indicator that we have left the bridge, jumped into the river of our emotions, and are being swept away by the current.

Have you ever had this experience? You ask someone who is obviously upset how they are doing, and receive an abrupt, "I'm fine!" You know that they are anything but "fine," but they do not seem able or interested to share their concern. When I hear the "I'm fine" response from someone I sense to be upset, I think of the acronym FINE: "Feelings In Need of Expression." FINE is a reminder that feelings need to be expressed. They need to move. They need to flow. We need to observe, acknowledge, and feel them, while standing on the bridge of our faith, the bridge of our spiritual life, which transcends and protects us from the strong, inevitable ebbs and flows of our emotions.

▶ Thought

What do you think of the idea that emotional resiliency is not so much an innate trait, as a skill that can be learned?

What are your thoughts about the concept that our emotions are like a river that flows under the bridge of our faith and spirituality?

▶ Word

In this reflection is a list of warning signs for the potential loss of emotional wellness. I invite you to talk with someone about your own warning signs that your emotional wellness is feeling compromised.

Several ideas for strengthening emotional resiliency are mentioned in this reflection. What are some practices or habits that strengthen your emotional resiliency? Might you want to speak with someone about adopting some of these practices?

▶ Deed

Paul urges us not to let the sun go down on our anger. Do you ever hold on to anger for days, or are you able to work through it? Why or why not? What do you do to release anger in a healthy way, so as not to get stuck in it?

Are you being swept away by your emotions right now? What can you do to climb "back on the bridge" so you don't get pulled down into those emotions or pull someone else down with you?

Reflection 5

The Collect for Purity

A beautiful prayer begins the celebration of the Eucharist in the Episcopal Church. Included in the first English Book of Common Prayer in 1549, it has been in every edition of Prayer Book since. The prayer is known as the Collect for Purity. We began our retreat with this prayer, and I include it again here because it has much to teach us about emotional wellness.

> Almighty God, to you all hearts are open, all desires known, and from you no secrets are hid: Cleanse the thoughts of our hearts by the inspiration of your Holy Spirit, that we may perfectly love you, and worthily magnify your holy Name; through Christ our Lord. Amen. (BCP, 355)

There are two essential truths embedded in this prayer. The first is that God is a loving God who desires a fully open, honest, and authentic connection with us. And it is, in fact, because of God's transformative love that we *can* be fully open, honest, and authentic in our relationship with God. On an interpersonal level, when we do not trust someone to be loving and accepting, we will not reveal our whole selves to them. We will instead reveal only what we think that person wants to know about us or we feel safe to reveal. When we pray the Collect for Purity we are saying that we are going to put "our whole selves in," to open our hearts and our lives fully to God.

This prayer appears at the beginning of worship for good reason: it sets the framework for everything else that follows. It says we are not just here, physically present for worship, but that we are here to open up our whole selves. It says that we intend to hold nothing back, feeling no need to hide any part of ourselves.

All Hearts Are Open

How the Grinch Stole Christmas by Dr. Seuss is the story of a Grinch who cannot stand to see the townspeople celebrating a warm and loving Christmas. He conspires against the people and tries to transform their Christmas joy into sadness. Eventually, it is the Grinch who is transformed in the story, but before this occurs there is a wonderful description of his cold-heartedness. We are told that his heart was "two sizes too small." The Grinch's heart was constricted and closed and he could not stand the sound and sight of people whose hearts were open and warm.

A closed heart is usually a heart that has been hurt in some way. Perhaps it has become closed as a result of grief or loss. Perhaps it has become closed because of some kind of betrayal. Perhaps it has become closed due to loneliness. Whatever the cause, the Collect for Purity invites us to open our hearts so that our emotional and spiritual wellness can be restored.

What helps us to open our hearts when they are either partially or fully closed? In the story of the Grinch, it is the open and loving hearts of the townspeople that gradually expand and open his heart. So it is with us. The love of others, whether it be the love of a friend, partner, spouse, or congregation, is what opens our hearts. Such love is a sacrament, an outward and visible sign of God's abundant love for us.

All Desires Known

The line "all desires known" from the Collect for Purity reminds us that we need not hide anything from God. The issue is not whether God already fully knows all our desires, but rather whether we fully acknowledge all our desires. We are complex people and our desires are complex. Our egos are strong and, if we are honest, we know they have desires that contain some amount of greed, pride, and self-righteousness. Psychology has used the term "shadow" to describe the desires that we hide from ourselves and from others. The shadow is a good description for these desires because we often try to hide what we are not proud of, keeping them hidden in the shadows of our hearts and souls.

There is a reason that we say the prayer of confession in the context of our worship every Sunday. We are confessing the thoughts, words, and deeds that come from our egos and the shadow side of ourselves. The Collect for Purity invites us to acknowledge all of our desires, not so that we can be embarrassed or shamed, but so that those desires can be released and we can be healed. If I have a selfish desire to gossip and speak poorly of someone, I cannot be healed of that desire unless and until I am willing to acknowledge and confess it. Keeping our desires secret is always destructive and this is why the next line of the Collect for Purity addresses the power of secrets.

From You No Secrets Are Hid

After the Collect for Purity invites us to open our hearts and make all of our desires known, it goes on to invite us to hide no secrets from ourselves and from God. Rather than hiding our secrets, we are invited to confess our secrets and open our whole selves to God to be restored and reconciled with ourselves, our neighbor, and with God. Holding on to or hiding secrets will divide and alienate us from ourselves, one another, and from God. The word "secret" means "something not known, and something set apart." Secrets set us apart and keep us from knowing and being fully known. Some people hold secrets that they are afraid will distance themselves from others they love, if revealed. Chances are the secrets being hidden are already creating distance and only in opening up the secret can the healing begin and the distance begin to diminish.

As a culture we seem fascinated with secrets, whether it's the latest leak from the National Security Agency or the latest secret about a famous celebrity or athlete. We are especially fascinated when people go to extreme lengths to deny the truth, a truth that seems obvious to everyone but them. I can only assume that we are fascinated by these stories because we see in them a projection (albeit perhaps in extreme form) of ourselves and our own struggles to be honest people. Rather than expending energy wondering how a politician or celebrity could spin such a web of lies, perhaps a better use of our energy is to look in the mirror and examine our own lives for any secrets, big or small, that we may be keeping.

The twelve-step recovery movement says, "You are only as sick as your secrets." The powerful truth of this may not be quite so obvious at first. It's not just the content of the secret that is unhealthy. What actually creates the greatest amount of "dis-ease" is the emotional and spiritual energy it requires to keep the secret hidden. I believe that this is the wisdom within the Collect for Purity, and our praying this prayer opens us to stop hiding any secrets we may have.

If you have ever seen the face of a young child who has stolen a cookie from the cookie jar and is trying to conceal his guilt, you know how much energy it takes to hide a wrongdoing. It takes no less energy for adults to hide their secrets or wrongdoings. Adults, unfortunately, have just gotten much better at it.

When a secret exists within a relationship, a family, or a congregation, it always hurts and divides. Relationships, families, and congregations can go to great lengths to hide a problem, be it ethical misconduct, infidelity, domestic violence, verbal abuse, a "problem child," financial struggles, or an addiction to alcohol or other drugs. Without a word being said, everyone learns the dance of denial, even though they all carry around the knowledge that something is not right. This dance can last a long time, but it cannot last forever because the truth *always* breaks through in one way or another. The secret usually breaks through in the form of some symptom or dysfunction. Only later, when the secret is revealed, is the connection made to the dysfunction that it created.

Keeping destructive secrets is not an accurate description of what happens with secrets, because in reality, secrets keep us. They keep us from being fully alive and fully connected to God and to others. When a secret is revealed and confessed, healing and reconciliation can begin. Every religion has rites for the confession of sins and secrets, which provide a way for their release, and for healing to begin. Jesus said, "We're not keeping secrets, we're telling them; we're not hiding things, we're bringing them out into the open" (Mark 4:22, *The Message*).

It turns out that praying the Collect for Purity, this five-hundred-year-old prayer that invites us to open our hearts, acknowledge all of our desires, and hide no secrets, can do much to help us with our emotional, spiritual, and relational wellness.

▶ Thought

Have you ever thought about the words of the Collect for Purity in this light? What thoughts do you have now after reading this reflection?

What do you think about the statement from the twelve-step movement, "We are only as sick as our secrets"?

▶ Word

Share a story of a time when you have observed a secret hurting or destroying a relationship, family, or congregation.

Is there someone in your life with whom you would like to talk more openly? What would help you to take the first step in doing this?

▶ Deed

I invite you to pray the Collect for Purity every day for a week. Say it slowly and reflect on what God is inviting you to do in and through the words of this prayer.

The Collect for Purity talks about the importance of opening your heart. What is something you do that helps open your heart to others and to God? Is there anything more you would like to do to keep your heart open to others and to God?

Chapter 10

REFLECTING ON YOUR RETREAT

At this point you have completed most or all of the forty reflections that comprise this self-guided retreat. I truly hope this experience has provided you with a chance to step back from your everyday life and reflect on what matters most to you. Such honest self-reflection requires courage, and yet the potential benefits are immense.

There are two practices that are essential for ongoing wellness and they have been foundational to this retreat. Whatever else you take away from this retreat, I hope that you will remember these two practices, as they apply to wellness at all levels—personal, family, and community.

The first practice is that of *regular self-refection*. The potential for true wellness exists when we develop the capacity for honest self-reflection. It is in and through such self-reflection that the Spirit speaks to us the truth that we most need to hear. The practice of self-reflection is simply making time and room to hear what the Spirit is saying to us.

The second practice, essential to creating ongoing wellness, is the *courage to make different choices* in our lives. Once we have discerned the truth that the Spirit is speaking to us we need to summon courage from within to make the necessary changes by creating different thoughts, words, and/or deeds.

These two truths regarding self-reflection and creating change through making different choices have been foundational to this self-guided retreat. As you seek to internalize these practices, be patient with yourself, knowing that through practice it will eventually become second nature to self-reflect and make changes as needed. If you continue to pay attention to this way of being it can become foundational in your life.

What else have you learned about yourself from this self-guided retreat? What do you want to be sure to continue to pay attention to, in order to create and maintain a sense of balance and wellness in your life? By now you know that the Spirit is always whispering to us regarding what needs attention in our lives, our relationships, and our congregations or other community organizations.

You may find it helpful at times to return to a specific section of this self-guided retreat when you feel a need to reflect on one particular area of wellness. Rereading some of the reflections and reflecting on the questions may spark new ideas for growth and change. Even though you may have read the reflections and questions before, when you read them at some future point you will be in a different place in your life, and therefore what speaks to you will be different.

If you have worked through this self-guided retreat on your own, you might want to consider the possibility of doing all or part of the retreat with a group of others who are committed to reflecting on and creating more wellness in their lives. There is always much wisdom and thus inspiration in a group of people working both separately and together on living into the abundant life that the Spirit intends for each one of us.

Finally, remember that the most important insights to hold on to from the experience of this self-guided retreat are your own. Your "Aha!" moments, your connections with the Spirit and with your deeper self are invaluable. Anything you have read in this book is secondary to any insights and learnings the Spirit has opened up for you.

Send Us Now into the World in Peace

Near the end of worship each Sunday, right after Communion, many Episcopalians pray the following words together: "Send us now into the world in peace, and grant us strength and courage to love and serve you with gladness and singleness of heart" (BCP, 365). As we come to the end of this retreat, these are good words for us to pray and reflect upon together. We will see that they describe both the steps needed to deepen our faith and wellness, and the fruit that will be made manifest in our lives and in our relationships when we do so.

We ask God to send us into the world in peace as we leave the liturgy each week. Peace is one of those words that we use so often that it is easy to overlook what a powerful and transformative concept it is. In his final conversation with his disciples, Jesus tells them, "Peace I leave with you; my peace I give to you. I do not give to you as the world gives. Do not let your hearts be troubled, and do not let them be afraid" (John 14:27). This is indeed what God wishes to give to us. The paradox is that while we want this more than anything, we have to remind ourselves to receive and nurture the gift of God's peace on a daily basis.

The concept of God's peace is so central to our life of faith that we pause in the middle of our liturgy each week to offer the "peace of the Lord" to each other. This simple and profound gesture is at the heart of our spiritual, emotional, and relational wellness. This gesture is not just something to be done during our liturgy, but something to be carried into our lives and practiced on a regular basis. Each of us has countless opportunities to offer the "peace of the Lord" to people every day, not necessarily with those literal words, but certainly in and through our thoughts, words, and deeds.

In order to share the peace of the Lord, we need to know the peace of the Lord in our own hearts, souls, and minds. Through regular spiritual practices, we need to breathe this peace deeply into our being. We receive a blessing at the end of worship each week that contains the words, "May the peace of God which passes all understanding be upon you." This peace may be beyond our understanding, but it is well within our understanding to know some of the things we need to do to grow and maintain this peace in our lives.

It is common to hear people talk about "peace of mind." Throughout this retreat we have expanded this concept to include peace of soul, peace of heart, and peace of strength or body. The peace that God desires to give us is indeed peace in all four of these dimensions of our being. As you conclude this book I hope you will continue to reflect upon the ongoing choices that you feel called to make to continue to breathe this peace into your life.

Strength and Courage

In the post-Communion prayer, we ask God to "grant us strength and courage." There is no doubt that God grants us strength and courage. It is up to us to do our part to discern what it means for each of us to receive and grow in this strength and courage. We know the way to grow stronger physically is to exercise our bodies, and the need for exercise applies to all dimensions of wellness in our lives as well. If we wish to build strength in the areas of spirituality, handling emotions, relationships, or the intellect, we need to exercise our "muscles" in those areas on a regular basis. Hopefully you can see a difference in yourself after having exercised those "muscles" during this retreat.

Courage is also a certain kind of strength. In this case, it refers to inner strength. The word "courage" comes from the same root meaning as the word "heart," but it clearly speaks of a strength of spirit and a strength of mind as well. We talk about the "courage of one's convictions," which is the courage required to do what one feels called to do even when the act would be unpopular or difficult. In fact, remaining intentional about deepening our faith and wellness takes much courage. It takes both the courage of our convictions and the courage to walk this less-traveled road, this path that takes us through the narrow gate.

To Love and Serve

When we pray that God would grant us strength and courage, we are asking for those gifts in order to do something very specific: to love and serve. There is no better way, no more concrete way to exercise our faith than by loving and serving God and our neighbor. Loving and serving others is how we nurture wellness in all areas of our lives, and at the same time, love and a willingness to serve are the fruits that flow from our lives when we are experiencing wellness.

With Gladness and Singleness of Heart

Many people have been exposed to a negative or fear-based approach to Christian spirituality that emphasizes fear, shame, and guilt. This fear-based approach may produce some behavioral change in the short run, but it rarely produces the true spiritual fruit of gladness, peace, joy, love, and service in the long run.

I envision God calling us to a life of wholeness and wellness from a place of love, not fear or guilt. It is an abundant life that God desires for us (John 10:10). To align all areas of our lives with God's intentions is to experience joy and gladness for ourselves, and at the same time it means we will also share joy and gladness with our neighbor. We commit to this life-long journey of deepening faith and wellness not because we have to, or not because we should, but because we want to—and we want to with gladness and singleness of heart. The idea of singleness of heart is what we mean when we talk about making our faith the living compass of our lives. There are many compasses that compete to guide our lives and there are many forces that act upon our hearts. To maintain singleness of heart requires tremendous discipline. It is an ideal that we are constantly striving for and an ideal that we are constantly being pulled toward by the one loving God, whose deepest desire is that "my joy may be in you, and that your joy may be complete" (John 15:11).

Faith, Wellness, and Bike Maintenance

I love to bike. I ride my bicycle whenever I can, as I find that it is truly re-creative for my heart, soul, mind, and body. One winter I decided I wanted to learn more about how to keep my bike tuned up, so I enrolled in a six-week bike maintenance class. Taking our bikes to the class each week, we applied an important concept regarding bicycle "wellness." We did not take this class because our bikes were broken, but because we wanted to become more proactive in learning how to keep them tuned and working well. I learned how to lubricate the chain, tighten the wheel spokes, adjust the brakes, and change a flat tire. Most importantly, I learned that it is easier and wiser to do the maintenance than it is to fix something when it is broken.

Your participating in this retreat is similar to my bike maintenance class. You have learned and applied some proactive ideas regarding faith and wellness to your life. Hopefully, you have found your life to be a little more "in tune" based on what you have learned and applied. The connection between your faith and your wellness, like bikes, requires ongoing tuning and maintenance. Having a robust faith and living a life of wellness are not a final destination, but an ongoing journey and work in progress.

I intend to take the bike maintenance class again soon because there will always be more to learn, and next time I will work on a different part of my bike. Similarly, you might want to experience this retreat again in six months or a year for the same reasons: there is always more to learn and you might desire to work on different areas of your wellness.

Please visit our LivingCompass.org website to subscribe to our "Weekly Words of Wellness" email column and to learn about other resources that can support you and your congregation on your ongoing journey of wellness.

It has been a joy and an honor to ride this part of the journey with you. May we hold each other in the Light as we continue to discover, discern, and walk the way, the truth, and the life that God has in store for us.

THE LIVING COMPASS
SELF-ASSESSMENT TOOL

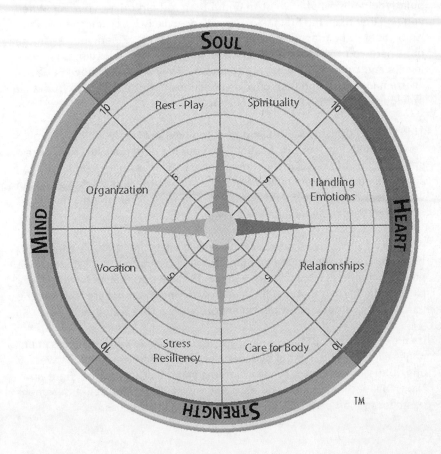

Once you have your number between 0 and 10 from the self-assessment provided for each section of the compass, you can shade in that section based on that number. At the center of the compass is the number 0; the number 5 is halfway out, and 10 is at the outer edge. Use a pencil, pen, or crayons to shade in the various sections. Your scores are not "good" or "bad," nor are they "strong" or "weak." They are simply a reflection of what you have been paying attention to in your life.

▶ You Are Here

If you find yourself walking around in an unfamiliar city or airport, at some point you will probably want to find a map to help orient yourself. When you find that map, the first thing you will most likely look for is the "You Are Here" dot on the map. Once you know where you are, then you can figure out where you want to go and how best to get there. Navigational software in cars and cell phones work the same way. They begin by showing us our "current location" and then offer us directions to our destination from that previously established "current location."

This Living Compass Self-Assessment Tool will provide you with a similar "You Are Here" or "current location" for your life right now. It is a very present-day snapshot of your state of balance, wholeness and wellness. If you completed this assessment three months ago your results might have been very different than today. And likewise, your results three months from right now would probably be different as well.

Another way to think about your self-assessment is that it simply shows you what you have been paying attention to the most in your life. Whatever we pay attention to is what will grow in life. Think of your life as a garden. The parts of the garden that you have been watering the most are thriving; the parts you have not been watering are probably a little wilted right now.

It's time to get started! Read each statement in the following self-assessment pages carefully and without over-thinking. Put down the number between 0 and 10 that best reflects the truth of this statement in your life right now. Next, follow the directions on each page for filling in the self-assessment compass tool on page 155. We hope you enjoy the process.

▶ Spirituality Assessment

The word "spirituality" comes from the same root as the word "breath." This is seen in the word "respiration," another word for breath. Spirituality is that which gives breath, that which animates a person's life. For Christians, spirituality refers to the way in which our faith animates our lives. Our faith and beliefs can be expressed in written statements such as a creed. Our spirituality is expressed in the way we live our lives.

Never	Sometimes	Half of the Time	Most of the Time	Always
0 1	2 3	4 5 6	7 8	9 10

I have a strong sense of God's presence in my life.   _____

I am satisfied with my spiritual life.   _____

I feel well connected to a faith community and feel supported
by that community.   _____

I read the Bible or some other kind of spiritual reading
on a regular basis.   _____

The way I live my life is consistent with my faith and values.   _____

I have a deep sense of gratitude for the many blessings in my life.   _____

People who know me well would describe me as very compassionate.   _____

I am comfortable talking about my faith/spirituality with others.   _____

I have spiritual practices and/or an active prayer life that are
a regular part of my life.   _____

People who know me well would describe me as a person of
faith, or as a very spiritual person.   _____

TOTAL   _____

Divide by 10   _____

*Transfer this number to the Spirituality wedge
of the self-assessment compass tool on page 155.*

▶ Rest and Play Assessment

People often feel guilty when they take time to have fun, goof off, take a nap, or just play, but our bodies need to be recharged just like our phones and computers. Healthy sleep, fun time with family and friends, unscheduled and "unplugged" time, all help us lower the stress hormone cortisol, and feel refreshed and ready to go.

Never		Sometimes		Half of the Time			Most of the Time			Always
0	1	2	3	4	5	6	7	8	9	10

I use some of my rest time as Sabbath time, to intentionally
renew my relationship with God. _____

I take time to recreate and renew myself on a regular basis. _____

People who know me well would say I am a fun-loving person. _____

I have at least one hobby or interest that I am passionate about,
and I make time for it on a regular basis. _____

I love to try new things, new activities, and new ways to have fun. _____

I am satisfied with how much sleep I get on a regular basis. _____

I laugh a great deal. _____

I regularly have enough time to tend to all the important
relationships and the important tasks in my life. _____

I am satisfied that I am not overly connected to email,
TV, internet, laptop, and other technology. _____

I take all of the vacation and time off I am due each year, and
don't stress about work while I am away from work.

(Or I am retired, or not working outside the home right now,
and I am completely satisfied with that.) _____

TOTAL _____

Divide by 10 _____

*Transfer this number to the Rest and Play wedge
of the self-assessment compass tool on page 155.*

▶ Vocation Assessment

Our vocation is related to our sense of life purpose and our core values, and it can be expressed in our career, education, and/or volunteer work. If the hours we spend at work / school / volunteer work are aligned with our vocation / purpose / values, then we will experience wellness in what we do. If not, we have an opportunity to reconsider other ways we can express our vocation that may better provide wholeness and wellness in our lives.

Never		Sometimes		Half of the Time			Most of the Time		Always	
0	1	2	3	4	5	6	7	8	9	10

I have a clear sense of the gifts and talents that God has given me. _____

I make good use of the gifts and talents that God has given me in the work / school / service I do. _____

I am satisfied with how my work / school /service is balanced with my personal life. _____

I have others in my life who enjoy the same kind of work / school / service I do. _____

I welcome opportunities to learn new things that will enhance my work / school / service. _____

My work / school / service is congruent with my faith, beliefs, and values. _____

I would feel confident making a change in my work / school / service if I needed to. _____

I am happy with the pay / grades / recognition I receive for my work / school / service. _____

I am proud of myself when it comes to my work / school / service. _____

I have a clear sense of purpose and direction in my work / school / service. _____

TOTAL _____

Divide by 10 _____

Transfer this number to the Vocation wedge of the self-assessment compass tool on page 155.

▶ Organization Assessment

Whether your organizational challenges deal with time, money, your environment, or planning, you are not alone. Many people find that disorganization tends to look like a vicious circle—we're not organized, which causes stress, the stress causes us to pay attention to other things so we don't get organized, and this causes more stress. By choosing what you would you like to pay more attention to, you can begin to minimize the vicious circle.

Never		Sometimes		Half of the Time			Most of the Time			Always
0	1	2	3	4	5	6	7	8	9	10

I have a budget and a savings and/or retirement plan and I stick
to them. _____

My Christian faith strongly guides my relationship with money
and material possessions. _____

I am on time for appointments, meetings and social events. _____

I keep track of my personal belongings such as my keys, wallet, purse,
or other important items such as personal papers, and can get my hands
on them immediately at any time. _____

At the end of the day I usually feel like I accomplished everything
that I had hoped to get done that day. _____

I regularly make time to plan ahead for things so that I rarely have
to rush around at the last minute to get ready. _____

People who know me well would describe me as well organized. _____

My finances are well organized, which means the following:
I have a pretty close estimate of the balance in my bank accounts
at all times, I pay all bills on time, I have savings goals and keep them,
I organize tax information and file my taxes on time each year. _____

If an unexpected visitor surprises me and wants to enter my home,
car, or office, I don't have to worry about how messy it is. _____

I regularly go through my closet, basement, garage, attic, and drawers
and get rid of things I don't need. _____

TOTAL _____

Divide by 10 _____

Transfer this number to the Organization wedge
of the self-assessment compass tool on page 155.

▶ Care for the Body Assessment

Our culture puts a great deal of emphasis on physical wellness and body image. The two extremes of either obsessing about our bodies, or neglecting them, are clearly something we want to avoid. It can be challenging, but essential for our long-term health, to find a balanced approach for the care and nurturing of our physical wellness.

Never		Sometimes		Half of the Time		Most of the Time			Always
0	1	2	3	4	5	6	7	8	9	10

I am very satisfied with the amount of regular physical activity I get. _____

I treat my body as "a temple of the Holy Spirit" within me (1 Cor. 6:19). _____

I go to the doctor and dentist for regular physicals / checkups
and also seek help as soon as a problem arises. _____

I am comfortable with my sexuality. _____

I make conscious, intentional decisions about what I eat and drink. _____

I am very satisfied with my current weight. _____

I am satisfied with my use of tobacco. _____

I am satisfied with the decisions that I make about the use of alcohol
and/or other mood-altering drugs. _____

I am able to ignore what the culture tells me regarding how
I should look in terms of weight or appearance and instead
can decide for myself what is healthy and best for me. _____

I eat a balanced diet and overall feel good about the relationship
I have with food. _____

TOTAL _____

Divide by 10 _____

*Transfer this number to the Care for the Body wedge
of the self-assessment compass tool on page 155.*

▶ Stress Resiliency Assessment

The word "resiliency" means to "bounce back." Our modern lives are filled with frustrations and pressures—we just call it stress. Stress is actually a physical and emotional response to any particular situation. It can be short- or long-term, but if it is constantly elevated, stress can make you more vulnerable to health problems. The good news is that we can develop skills to become more resilient, to help us bounce back from the inevitable stress that life brings us at times.

Never		Sometimes		Half of the Time			Most of the Time			Always
0	1	2	3	4	5	6	7	8	9	10

My life has been free of any major life changes, planned or unplanned, over the last two years. ____

When I am stressed or in the midst of transition, I turn to God and my spiritual life to give me strength and resiliency. ____

I seek support from others, rather than isolating myself, in times of stress or transition. ____

People who know me well would describe me as a person with little stress in my life. ____

I have the tools necessary to handle a major life challenge. ____

I think I am resilient—I "bounce back" well when it comes to stressful situations. ____

I refrain from using alcohol, drugs, or food to numb or medicate myself when I am stressed. ____

I have been free from any feelings of stress throughout the last month. ____

I have been free from any physical symptoms that may be related to stress over the last month. ____

I refrain from making decisions, such as overcommitting and putting high expectations on myself, that self-inflict high levels of intensity and stress in my life. ____

TOTAL ____

Divide by 10 ____

Transfer this number to the Stress Resiliency wedge of the self-assessment compass tool on page 155.

▶ Relationships Assessment

Relationships don't just "happen": we co-create them with others. Remember, everyone can learn skills that will improve the quality of their relationships. The grass is always greener where you water it, so how would you like to see your relationship garden grow?

Never		Sometimes		Half of the Time			Most of the Time		Always
0	1	2	3	4	5	6	7	8	9	10

I am satisfied with the relationships I have with my parents, siblings, and extended family.   _____

I am satisfied with the quality of the relationships I have with my spouse, partner, children, and/or close friends.   _____

The teachings of my Christian faith are a conscious influence and guide on how I relate to others in my life.   _____

I have forgiven family and friends for past or present hurts.   _____

I am satisfied with the way and frequency with which I keep in touch with family and friends.   _____

In my relationships with family and friends I am satisfied that there is a good balance between give and take.   _____

My family and friends know me in a deeper and more intimate way than people who are more casual friends and acquaintances.   _____

My family and friends would say that spending time with them is a high priority for me, and that my actions show this.   _____

I have several long-term friendships that have lasted many years.   _____

I am able to resolve conflict in a productive way with family and friends. We are able to talk about conflict so that it does not fester.   _____

TOTAL   _____

Divide by 10   _____

Transfer this number to the Relationships wedge of the self-assessment compass tool on page 155.

▶ Handling Emotions Assessment

We have a choice when it comes to responding to statements, questions, circumstances, and events, and can grow to become more centered. When we have greater control over our emotions, we do not have to react mindlessly, but can choose a response and an accompanying healthy emotional expression.

Never	Sometimes	Half of the Time	Most of the Time	Always
0 1	2 3	4 5 6	7 8	9 10

I avoid using alcohol and other possibly addictive behaviors to deal with my emotions.   _____

During the last month I have been able to refrain from hurting others by giving them the "silent treatment" or by being irritable, critical, or angry with them.   _____

When I am emotionally upset, I often turn to God or to prayer to help me re-center myself.   _____

I have been free of any feelings of anxiety or excessive worry in the last month.   _____

People who are close to me would say that I handle my emotions well. _____

I do not feel responsible for other people's emotions.   _____

I can feel and express the full range of emotions (sadness, fear, joy, laughter).   _____

When someone I care about is upset, I am comfortable listening and really being present to them. (I don't jump in to fix or give advice, and I don't walk away or detach myself.)   _____

I am able to stay centered in situations where someone else might be perceived as "pushing my buttons."   _____

In the last month I have been free of any feelings of depression and/or despair.   _____

TOTAL   _____

Divide by 10   _____

*Transfer this number to the Handling Emotions wedge
of the self-assessment compass tool on page 155.*

A GUIDE FOR USE
IN CONGREGATIONS

There is great benefit in doing this self-guided retreat on your own in private. There are several additional benefits to doing this retreat in community with others. You may find that you are able to clarify your thoughts and intentions as you have the chance to speak them out loud to a community of others who are seeking to more fully integrate their spirituality and wellness. And there is always so much wisdom to be learned from what others share in the group.

Congregations are ideal communities within which this self-guided retreat can be used. Communities of faith are by definition committed to helping people more fully integrate their faith with their day-to-day life. While currently there is much focus in our culture on the topic of wellness, faith communities have been centers of faith and wellness for thousands of years.

Offering wellness programs such as this self-guided retreat in a congregation provides an opportunity for members of a congregation to connect and know each other at a deeper, more personal level. Whenever I facilitate a Living Compass retreat or small group program in a congregation, participants report that they are delighted to get to know the true joys and concerns in each others' lives, and in the process their church community becomes even more important to them.

Many congregations have also discovered that hosting wellness programs, such as those provided by Living Compass, opens up opportunities to reach out to their surrounding neighborhoods. Members of a congregation find that they are more likely to invite their friends who do not have a church to attend a wellness program with them than they are to invite them to worship with them on Sunday morning. Thus, more members of the community are introduced to what church can offer them.

With this in mind, here are some ways in which this self-guided retreat can be used in a congregation.

  ◆ It can be used as a text for an adult education class. Any or all
    of the reflections for Living Compass' eight areas of wellness
    could be read and discussed by the members of the class.

◆ It can be used as a text for a seasonal program, such as Advent or Lent. Due to the length of the season, one of the eight areas of wellness covered in this book could be the focus for such a program.

◆ It can be used as a gathering meditation with a group from the congregation that already meets regularly, such as a vestry, a men's or women's group, a parents' group, or a Bible study. Each meeting could include reading and discussing a reflection from this book.

◆ It can also be used as a separate, stand-alone retreat offering. Depending on the length of the retreat, several reflections from one of the eight areas of wellness could be read and discussed. Another retreat format could include one or two reflections from each of the four points of the Living Compass: heart, soul, strength, and mind. The retreat could also provide time for participants to spend quiet time alone reflecting on the chosen reflections, and/or taking time to record their thoughts and responses in a journal.

A foundational idea that runs throughout this book is that wellness flows from and is grounded in our relationship with God and with one another. For this reason, however one makes use of this book, it is ideally suited for use in a congregational setting.

ACKNOWLEDGMENTS

Wellness is both grounded and most fully expressed in community. The writing of this book has also been grounded in community. I have been blessed by the support and influence of many family members, friends, colleagues, and congregations. Each of their voices has shaped my voice and therefore shaped what I have written in these pages. I am thankful for each of them: for the part they played in the creation of the Living Compass ministry, and in the creation of this book.

First, I want to thank Ab and Nancy Nicholas for their generous support of the Living Compass Faith and Wellness Initiative. Through our work together we have become dear friends, and without their support, Living Compass and this book would not be possible. Ab and Nancy embody the principles that are taught in this book as well as anyone I know, in their own lives and in the way they give back to the community.

Jim and Libby Wigdale have also been strong supporters of our ministry, as well as wonderful friends, from the beginning. They, too, model wellness in their lives and are thus inspirations to me. I am especially grateful for Jim's constant reminder not to sacrifice my own wellness as I work to help others with theirs.

My ministry has been within the Episcopal Diocese of Milwaukee for the last twenty-seven years and this book has grown out of my experiences there. I am especially grateful for the support that Bishop Steven Miller has given me over the last ten years. The Reverend Gary Manning has been part of the Living Compass community from the very beginning, and the church where he serves as rector, Trinity Episcopal Church in Wauwatosa, served as living laboratory for the development of many ideas in this book. Many other clergy from the Diocese of Milwaukee have also provided important support and feedback for my ministry, including Carla McCook, Steve Teague, Jan Kwiatkowski, Seth Dietrich, Paula Harris, Lisa Saunders (now in the Diocese of Texas), Debra Trakel, and Deborah Woolsey (now in the Diocese of Southern Ohio). Thanks to all of you.

The Reverend Rick Oberheide and the people of Grace Episcopal Church in Sheffield, Alabama also provided early and important support for the Living Compass ministry, for which I am grateful. Rick and I have been sharing ideas about the integration of faith and wellness for over thirty years that were the seeds for this ministry and book.

I am most grateful for the support of Bishop Jeffrey Lee of the Diocese of Chicago, and the wonderful diocesan staff, who have all been key partners in the development of the ideas in this book. The recently opened Nicholas Center, located at St. James Commons in the Diocese of Chicago, will serve as the national training center for the Living Compass Faith and Wellness Initiative.

There are several other people who have been an important part of the community that has made this book possible and I am thankful for them all. Edith Braeger, who works with us at Living Compass, is a lead coach and trainer with our Living Compass for Parents Initiative and has been a sounding board all along. She wears many hats for us and her contagious enthusiasm is a gift to all who work with her. The Reverend Shannon Ferguson Kelly and the Reverend Carol Peterson have both joined our Living Compass team recently, and I am most grateful for the ways in which they are enhancing and expanding both our materials and our ministry. I wish to thank Matthew Ellis, CEO of the National Episcopal Health Ministries, for his support of Living Compass. Karin Jamel has also done an amazing job in bringing all of the Living Compass materials to life.

The YMCA of Greater Milwaukee was one of the early supporters of the Living Compass program. I am especially grateful to Janet McMahon and Julia Gray for sharing their wisdom and commitment to whole-person wellness, and for helping me to see the potential for this program.

As a first-time author, I am especially grateful for the support of Nancy Bryan, the editor for this book. She walked me through the process, one step at a time, and provided invaluable editorial insight regarding the original manuscript. I am grateful for the support that she, copyeditor Vicki Black, and Church Publishing have provided to make this book possible.

I extend my deepest gratitude to the most important community in my life—my wife and family. Holly and I have been partners in marriage for thirty-six years and are now blessed to be partners in the Living Compass ministry as well. She, along with our adult children and their partners and now a grandson, are the community that has influenced and shaped me the most when it comes to living a life that is grounded in faith, wellness, and wholeness. What I know about love, healing, commitment, character, and an encompassing spirituality I have learned in community with Holly and our family.

Finally, thank you to the individuals and congregations who will take the time to read and use this book as a reflection tool, a compass, to assist you on your journey toward a spiritually grounded wellness. It is an honor to walk with you on this journey as a fellow traveler. Together, we are blessed to be a community seeking to live into the wholeness that is God's gift to each and every one of us now and forever.